LANGUAGE AND LITERACY SERIES

Dorothy S. Strickland and Celia Genishi, SERIES EDITORS

ADVISORY BOARD: RICHARD ALLINGTON, DONNA ALVERMANN, KATHRYN AU, BERNICE CULLINAN, COLETTE DAIUTE, ANNE HAAS DYSON, CAROLE EDELSKY, JANET EMIG, SHIRLEY BRICE HEATH, CONNIE JUEL, SUSAN LYTLE

(Continued)

Room for Talk

TEACHING AND LEARNING IN A MULTILINGUAL KINDERGARTEN

Rebekah Fassler

FOREWORD BY CELIA GENISHI

Teachers College, Columbia University
New York and London

Published by Teachers College Press, 1234 Amsterdam Avenue, New York, NY 10027

Portions of Chapters 1, 6, and 8 reprinted from *Early Childhood Research Quarterly, 13*, Rebekah Fassler, "Room for Talk: Peer Support for Getting into English in an ESL Kindergarten," pp. 379–409, Copyright 1998, with permission from Elsevier Science.

Library of Congress Cataloging-in-Publication Data

Fassler, Rebekah.
    Room for talk : teaching and learning in a multilingual kindergarten / Rebekah Fassler; foreword by Celia Genishi.
       p. cm.—(Language and literacy series)
    Includes bibliographic references and index.
    ISBN 0-8077-4376-3 (cloth : alk paper)—ISBN 0-8077-4375-5 (pbk : alk paper)
    1. Linguistic minorities—Education (Early childhood)—United States. 2. Language arts (Kindergarten)—United States. 3. English language—Study and teaching—United States—Foreign speakers. 4. Multicultural education—United States.
I. Title. II. Language and literacy series (New York, N.Y.)

LC3731 .F39 2003
372.21'8—dc21   2003048444

ISBN 0-8077-4375-5 (paper)
ISBN 0-8077-4376-3 (cloth)

Contents

Foreword

How do kindergartners make sense of their worlds? According to Rebekah Fassler, some kindergartners are able to rely on grown-ups and one or more friends to help them make the world sensible and pleasurable. In the pages that follow, we meet kindergartners who are fluent speakers of a variety of languages—none of them English—at the start of the school year. Over a period of six months, Rebekah, as participant observer, begins to make sense of the young learners' entry into the world of English, where each learner takes on differing roles, just for starters: listener, speaker, humorist, game player, story sharer. The author is a researcher with acute, child-sensitive eyes and ears, and she richly describes how six children, Inga, Jerry, Pierre, Robert, Tracy, and Yakov, along with their peers and teacher, progress through time. Drawing on detailed notes and transcripts, Rebekah builds a stage on which the children and teacher interact, each in a unique style that marks a path into schooling in English.

In Mrs. Barker's public school kindergarten classroom, talk in any language is allowed and often ennobled by responsive collaborators. Collaboration among schoolchildren and their teachers is a common goal in many classrooms, though it may seem unlikely to occur in a room like Mrs. Barker's, where she is the only fluent English speaker. But collaboration it is, as participants negotiate to create meaning together. Some of the negotiations focus on exactly what a child means—does Pierre mean *brown* and not *red*? Is the conversational topic Tracy's brother or the health of the teacher's baby? Mrs. Barker and her kindergartners become especially skilled at keeping conversations alive until meaning is shared.

The number of children in North American classrooms who are English language learners in need of someone like Mrs. Barker is rapidly increasing, as is the number of different languages children use in individual classrooms. In response to this changing multilingual and multicultural population, educators have designed a range of programs, from those that are bilingual, involving the frequent use of English and one other language, to English immersion, often called "sink or swim" since there are no formalized ways of supporting English language learners in these rooms. The program in Mrs. Barker's school is unusual in that it places *only* English language learners in an ESL classroom. How teacher and children learn from and teach each other in this setting—how they capitalize on each other's knowledge and strengths—is the core of Rebekah's insightful and important research story. There is a complex web of interactions throughout the book that emerge from that most human of intentions—the intention to communicate while making sense of the world. And though we might expect a heavy dose of "direct instruction" because the children's communicative skills in English are just budding, we find instead high doses of child and adult talk, enhanced by nonverbal resources. And we find challenges to traditional definitions of productive environments for learning language, in which native speakers of the target language are of greatest value.

Mrs. Barker approaches all her kindergartners as resourceful persons, "as whole personalities, with intentions, preferences, interests, feelings, and unique language-and-action ways," not as primarily "limited English proficient." Thus a multitude of conversations push children and teacher to rise to the communicative occasion, to make sense together via resources like facial expression, loudness, pantomime, the explanatory power of visible objects, and, of course, their affection for each other.

In short, as readers you can look forward to lively scenes where teacher and children collaborate to balance sense-making that incorporates scripted literacy and math content with sense-making that is playful, improvisatory language-and-action. You can also look forward to eight chapters of clear, thoughtful, and engaging prose that offers many strategies for teachers working with English language learners. Here is a compelling story full of learners to like and admire, who will now speak for themselves.

Celia Genishi
Teachers College, Columbia

Acknowledgments

This book had its roots in my dissertation research, undertaken in "Mrs. Barker's" ESL kindergarten. I am deeply grateful to "Mrs. Barker" for welcoming me into her classroom and to the children in her class for accepting my participation in their daily classroom life.

My interest in young English language learners and in classroom observation has spanned many years; throughout that period, I have been privileged to share my ideas and research with my teacher, friend, and colleague Celia Genishi. During my dissertation research, Leslie Williams also gave generously of her time and offered a valuable perspective on my work.

There are a number of colleagues and friends who have in a variety of ways contributed to the completion of this book. They are Connie Goldfarb, Barbara Weiserbs, Rachel Theilheimer, Anne Haas Dyson, Rene Parmar, Mary Ann Maslak, Shondel Nero, and Jerrold Ross.

Special thanks to Carol Chambers Collins, the acquisitions editor at Teachers College Press, for her incisive comments and pivotal suggestions at crucial points in the revision of this work. I am also grateful to Catherine McClure for her careful editing of the manuscript. Both her attention to detail and her thoughtful suggestions for the book as a whole were extremely helpful.

My nephew, David Fassler, provided a beautiful physical setting to launch major manuscript revisions. My children, Matthew and Rachel, have always been enthusiastic supporters of my professional life, and I thank them for their ongoing encouragement. I owe a special debt of gratitude to my husband, Norman, whose faith, love, wise counsel, and not least, sense of humor sustained me throughout this project. This book is dedicated to Norman.

1

Overview

In Mrs. Barker's ESL kindergarten in mid-December, Pierre and Gennady are coloring in Rudolph the Red-Nosed Reindeer cutouts and discussing colors. Pierre has just brought his cutout to the teacher to have the antlers put on.

TEACHER: I don't see his red nose.
PIERRE: (returning to his table for a crayon to color the nose, begins to chant) Red, red, red, red, red, red, red. (picks up a brown crayon) Red!
GENNADY: Pierre, give me orange.
PIERRE: Mrs. Barker say *red* like there. (indicates the brown highlights he is making)
GENNADY: (protesting) I need orange. (and pointing to Pierre's brown) I not need *gray*.
PIERRE: That's not *gray*!
TEACHER: (pointing at Pierre's reindeer) Pierre, I don't see red. Red.
GENNADY: I need red, I need red, I need red.
PIERRE: Mrs. Barker did dis one. (brown)
RESEARCHER: (to teacher about Gennady) He's looking for a red crayon. He's looking for a red crayon. And Pierre thinks red is brown.
TEACHER: Yakov . . . (who is sitting at another table) Give Gennady a red crayon.
GENNADY: (borrows a red crayon from Yakov and comes back to the table beaming)

Pierre, a Haitian-Creole and French speaker, and Gennady, a Russian speaker, were 2 of 31 second language (L2) learners in Mrs. Barker's class. (All names in the book are pseudonyms.) The children came from eight different language backgrounds and the teacher spoke only English. Just before the reindeer craft activity, Mrs. Barker led the children in a discussion of reindeers, in a demonstration of making reindeer cutouts, and in the singing of Rudolph the Red-Nosed Reindeer. Much color vocabulary was embedded in that introduction to the craft activity. Pierre, it seems, did not come through this particular experience accurately connecting the label *red* with the color red. But in other interactions with peers about 3 weeks later the connection seemed clarified.

> At Pierre's table, he and Gennady are discussing Power Rangers while playing with Legos. Ogusan (a Turkish speaker) leaves his table, where he has been working on a crafts activity, to argue with Pierre over who would be the much admired red Power Ranger in their play.
>
> OGUSAN: Look. I'm the red ranger.
> PIERRE: Me now red Power Ranger. Look. (pulls up his trouser legs so his bright red socks are visible) Me got red two shoes!
>
> A few minutes later:
>
> OGUSAN: (calls from his table) Pierre. Pierre. Pierre. Look! Look! I'm the red ranger. You see this? (Ogusan waves a piece of red tissue paper.)
> PIERRE: I'm the black Power Ranger. 'Je va' [I'm going to] fight!

In these latter interactions, the color red had a special relevance to Pierre and Ogusan, and, in negotiating play roles, they each used "personal" resources (reference to red socks and red paper) to make their point. The color label *red* was finally becoming a part of Pierre's *linguistic capital* (Ervin-Tripp, 1991). Moreover, in the rhythm of the argument, Pierre shifted from using *me* ("Me now red Power Ranger") as the subject to the grammatically correct *I* modeled by Ogusan ("I'm the black Power Ranger").

This book explores the positive resources for learning to use English and to make sense of curriculum that Pierre, his classmates, and their teacher brought to their classroom. That setting, from a traditional interactionist view of L2 acquisition, lacked a crucial ingredient for successful L2 learning—native English-speaking peers. In my role as a participant observer in their classroom during the first 6 months of the school year, I documented the range of contexts in which children came to use English and the efforts they and their teacher made to understand each other and be understood. In addition to looking at the class as a whole, I focused intensively on six case study children from three language backgrounds.

KEY CHALLENGES IN MULTILINGUAL CLASSROOMS

Pierre, Gennady, Ogusan, and their classmates were eager to communicate and were provided daily with many contexts, such as the reindeer activity, in which vocabulary introduced by Mrs. Barker could be used purposefully in social situations. The children also had abundant opportunity to interact with each other about topics of their own choosing, such as Power Rangers, as they talked during table activities and play.

Provision of authentic contexts for communication and encouragement of communication are considered important components of an ideal setting for L2 learning from an interactionist view of L2 acquisition. Peer communication from the beginning of the year was the hallmark of Mrs. Barker's classroom, but would that communication be rich enough to benefit the children as English language learners (ELLs)?

Balancing Contexts to Maximize L2 Learning

One key challenge faced by teachers in multilingual classrooms is to discover what kind of balance between teacher-fronted and peer-mediated activities will best support children's using English and learning to speak it better. Teachers often are concerned that in a situation where ELLs might often be each other's main peer resource for English, the poor quality of that English may limit its usefulness for language learning. Even with the support of concrete materials, Gennady and Pierre, each with gaps in their English vocabulary, were unable to provide each other with consistent support for correct color labels.

Moreover, although Pierre, Gennady, and Ogusan—all from different language backgrounds—needed English as a lingua franca, many of their classmates shared either Chinese or Russian as a home language. Teachers often worry that among cospeakers of a common home language it may be too tempting to stick with the comfortable home language in peer communication and delay using English altogether. In light of these concerns, should peer-mediated contexts such as play be considered potentially supportive for L2 learning, or be dismissed as downtime or time off task?

In classrooms where most children have a very limited repertoire of English from which to draw, exposure to the teacher's language, her *teacher talk*—her directives, her read-alouds, her deliberately tailored language to foster understanding—becomes increasingly crucial to ELLs. How can teachers help ELLs access and capitalize on such teacher talk in their efforts to learn and use English?

Establishing Intersubjectivity

Major exposure to teacher talk takes place during teacher-directed whole-group activities and in one-to-one teacher-child interactions. In such events, a second key challenge faced by monolingual teachers in multilingual classrooms is the challenge that Pierre and Gennady also faced—that of establishing *intersubjectivity*, a shared focus of attention and a knowledge that communicating partners "construe" or look upon the communicative situation the same way (Wells, 1981). In this chapter's introductory vignette, Pierre and Gennady established a shared focus of attention on colored crayons, but had difficulty reaching a shared understanding of just which colors they were talking about. They failed to establish intersubjectivity.

Many teachers, when confronted with linguistic diversity in the classroom, find themselves for the first time in a situation where they cannot take for granted what they can accomplish *through* oral language. In their efforts to make procedures and content understandable, they now always have to bear in mind making the medium of communication understandable too. How will the teacher and ELLs negotiate shared understandings not only of words, but of what kindergarten is all about?

WHAT MRS. BARKER'S CLASSROOM REPRESENTS

Self-contained ESL classrooms like Mrs. Barker's do not in theory represent an ideal L2 learning environment. However, they do represent one extreme on a continuum of linguistic diversity reflective of three growing trends that pose particular challenges to American early childhood teachers: (1) An increasing number of classrooms have children from home language backgrounds other than English. (2) The ratio of English language learners (ELLs) to native English speakers in those classrooms is increasing. (3) An increasing number of those classrooms have ELLs from a variety of home language backgrounds rather than from a single language background. Due partly to immigration patterns and complexities of urban school systems, these trends have become increasingly common, not only in the United States (Cummins, 1994; Kagan & Garcia, 1991), but also in

England (Ellis, 1983; Gregory, 1997) and Canada (Cumming, 2000; Dixon & Fraser, 1986).

In New York City alone during 2000–2001, 13.7 percent of the public school population of over 1.1 million children was identified as limited English proficient, with one-third of that population in kindergarten through second grade. Children came from almost 200 countries of origin, and from approximately 140 different language groups (Information, Reporting and Technology Services, 2001). In many schools, the heterogeneity of home language backgrounds mitigates against bilingual education as the support service of choice. For example, in New York City during 2000–2001, there were bilingual programs in only 11 of the 140 languages, serving 48.3 percent of the children; the rest of the children were served in settings where English was the sole language of instruction (Office of English Language Learners, 2001). Moreover, sometimes even when there was a "critical mass" of children on a grade level from a single language background, their parents might opt not to have them in a bilingual program. This was the case in Mrs. Barker's school, where the kindergarten parents opted out of bilingual education, even though there were enough Chinese-speaking children for bilingual kindergarten classes.

The issues of establishing intersubjectivity, helping children to access and capitalize on teacher talk, and balancing teacher-fronted and peer-mediated activities were magnified in Mrs. Barker's classroom, where the ratio of ELLs to native speakers and the heterogeneity of ELLs' language backgrounds were at an extreme end of the continuum. Thus, although Mrs. Barker's classroom was not typical or representative of multilingual classrooms, it provided an opportunity to see in a concentrated way the efforts, resources, and strategies a trained ESL teacher and her students would bring to bear in facing these challenges.

VIEWS ON PEER SUPPORT FOR L2 LEARNING

Pierre and his classmates found themselves in a setting very much like one of those described by Pica and her colleagues: "For many L2 learners, . . . opportunities for either extensive or wide-ranging interaction with NSs [native speakers] is all too infrequent and often simply impossible. . . . Thus, across a wide range of settings, . . . language learners are frequently and increasingly each other's resource for language learning" (Pica, Lincoln-Porter, Paninos, & Linnell, 1996, p. 60). Children like Pierre, Gennady, and their classmates, as well as monolingual teachers such as Mrs. Barker, have a pressing need to know how to capitalize on the positive resources for communication that they bring to this type of setting and on the positive aspects of the setting itself. Yet, the interactionist research offers no clear-cut conclusions on what the positive elements are. The greatest area of agreement is on the benefits of the one element that this setting lacks, an abundance of native English-speaking peers.

An Interactionist View

Many researchers would agree that in situations where peer interaction provides opportunities for ELLs to interact with native speakers, these interactions may contribute to L2 learning in a number of ways: ELLs have many sources of exposure to English besides their teacher and thus many more situations for talk that children may find authentic and intrinsically interesting (Enright, 1991). Such peer interactions often give children the opportunity to use forms of language that they would be unlikely to use in interacting with the teacher (Cazden, 1988). Language forms used for such purposes as nurturing, negotiating, persuading, arguing, and questioning expand what Ervin-Tripp (1991) has termed children's *linguistic capital*. Moreover, ELLs might find informal talking in L2 with peers less anxiety-provoking than interaction with the teacher, which often requires a more public and formal display of knowledge (Johnson, 1994). There are wide individual differences among language learners as to whether they prefer to interact more with a teacher or to tune in more to their peers (Genishi, 1989). For those who tend to avoid sustained interaction with teachers, the peer resource could be especially important.

There is also general agreement in the research literature about the kinds of support native English-speaking peers provide their ELL peers. In optimal situations for peer support, native English-speaking peers persistently initiate contact with ELLs. They also engage in some or all of the following behaviors that contribute to negotiation of shared meaning: They tailor their language to make it more understandable, often supplementing it with pantomime, gesture, facial expressions, sound effects, and demonstrations. They provide helpful feedback, expanding and rephrasing both their own and the ELLs' language in efforts to understand and be understood. Moreover, they push ELLs to refine their expression and to elaborate more, so as to clarify what they mean. There is evidence that some of these strategies can be deliberately taught even to preschoolers (Hirschler, 1991; Tabors, 1997).

All this assumes the presence of native English-speaking peers. But what benefits does peer interaction have for supporting L2 learning in classrooms where all the children are ELLs and where the children come from a multitude of language backgrounds? Almost all the research bearing on this question has been carried out either in bilingual classrooms, where children come from a common home language (L1) background, or in immersion classrooms, where the children share a common L1—which is a high-status language in the environment outside of school—and are learning L2 as a foreign language.

Pica (1994), in a review of research that addresses the relative benefits of peer interaction and teacher-fronted activities for L2 learning, concluded that the results are very complex and very context-specific. For instance, in a study of four bilingual kindergartens, Wong Fillmore (1982) found that frequent opportunities for peer interaction in small collaborative groups seemed to support language learning only in the classes with a balance of ELLs and native English speakers. R. Chesterfield, K. Chesterfield, Hayes-Latimer, and Chavez (1983) had a similar finding in bilingual preschool programs.

In French language immersion classrooms, students taking part in cooperative learning activities have often shown more motivation and less anxiety about speaking, and have engaged in more communication than if limited to interaction with the teacher in a large group (McGroarty, 1989; Swain & Lapkin, 1989). For these benefits to occur, the tasks the students engage in together must be interesting, have hands-on materials to help create a context for understanding, and require that students communicate with each other. One potential drawback is that although peer interaction may contribute to considerable fluency and confidence, the proficiency will always remain below that of native speakers. Swain (1985), however, has suggested that this makes peer interaction even more important—that teachers need to create situations for peer interaction that require students to push each other to refine their communication to be ever more clear and precise in their expression. She recommends that teachers look to peer interaction not only in terms of the potential for students to receive "comprehensible input" but also as an opportunity to make themselves understood by producing more refined and clear "comprehensible output."

The most optimistic statements about L2 learners promoting each other's L2 acquisition through peer interaction have come from research among adults. McGroarty (1989), in summarizing research primarily on adult peer interaction in cooperative learning situations as a context for L2 acquisition, reports that "analyses suggest that interaction with classmates, even if classmates are non-native speakers, does not induce students to commit more errors than they otherwise would, and, in fact, creates abundant natural contexts for self- and other-correction of errors which affect meaning, both semantic and morphosyntactic" (p. 138). Pica and colleagues (1996) also conclude that adult learners studied were to a limited extent able to modify what they said and how they responded to each other so as to make their meanings clearer, and were able to provide feedback that meaningfully supported clearer expression.

An Expanded Framework

Not enough is yet known about the possible peer support ELLs are able to offer each other in classrooms such as Mrs. Barker's. What makes her classroom different from both bilingual and immersion settings is the heterogeneity of language backgrounds. As I sought answers to my questions during the 6 months I spent as a participant observer in Mrs. Barker's classroom, I had to move beyond the traditional framework of interactionist theory that idealized resources, such as native English-speaking peers, that this classroom did not have. Moreover, the research relating to possible benefits of peer support in young children's classrooms has usually been couched in an either-or framework (Pica, 1994): Which is more supportive of L2 learning, a predominance of teacher-fronted activities or a predominance of opportunities for peer interaction? However, Johnson (1994) has recently suggested that the most support for L2 learning may come from environments where there is a balance of different participation structures for young L2 learners in classrooms. Such a balance would feature (1) a variety of whole group activities, in which interaction is between child and teacher and children receive major exposure to the teacher's English; (2) small-group activities in which children engage in peer interaction not directly mediated by the teacher; and (3) what Johnson terms *enhanced individual work*, in which children work on individual tasks, but can freely draw on their peers as resources in informal ways.

THE STUDY

In order to study the balance in Mrs. Barker's classroom between teacher-directed, whole-group activities and more informal contexts for talk, where children could shape their own interaction, I established myself from the very first day of school as an adult who "belonged" in the classroom, but not as a teacher. I adopted a *reactive* stance (Corsaro, 1981), not initiating interactions with the children, but responding when they made overtures to me. However, they soon learned that I didn't take on "teacher-like" roles such as helping with math tasks, dispensing discipline, or giving out materials. As one child put it, "She writes what children say."

Using a qualitative method, I took extensive field notes on oral communication in the classroom, as it naturally occurred during activities, events, and social situations throughout the school day. This was supplemented by selective audiotaping. To document efforts teacher and children made to negotiate shared meaning, that is, to understand each other and be understood, I tried to capture as fully as possible the context surrounding talk. Copies of charts, blackboard drawings, and children's work products associated with particular communicative events aided in keeping the context clear. In addition, I took notes on frequent informal talks with the teacher.

Initial data analysis involved typing up and expanding the observational field notes on a daily basis, and transcribing the audiotaped talk as soon as possible after taping. Speech transcription was usually limited to English, as I did not speak the other languages, except for limited French. However, when the speaker's voice could be identified, and when context notes were very clear and detailed, excerpts of audiotaped talk in home languages were translated. Even the brief glimpses that occasional translation provided made a difference in my appreciation of children's resources, attitudes, and behavior.

All field notes and transcriptions were entered into the computer. This made it possible to *chunk* together (copy and paste into one file) data from different times in a variety of ways for comparison. To preserve the context of communication, data were compared not by pulling speech fragments out of context, but by looking at speech as it was embedded in particular interactive situations. These situations I termed *episodes*. Most episodes were interactive situations in which participants were sharing or attempting to share a common focus of attention. Episodes were the basic units of analysis in the study, and always included information that conveyed the context of the interaction. Pierre's interactions with Gennady and Mrs. Barker during the reindeer activity comprise a combination of episodes in which the context of their talk is clearly conveyed.

By chunking episodes from the same type of activity over different days—for example, the series of regular events that constituted morning Group Time—I was able to discern patterns of participation and expectations for participation in different types of events. This helped to delineate the range of opportunities for communication in the classroom. For example, at Group Time, in contrast to Table Activities, most verbal interaction flowed between teacher and children, rather than between peers. The teacher usually controlled choice of topic and who had a turn to speak. Such features of the communicative situation defined the particular *participation structures* (Erickson & Shultz, 1981) for those activities.

At the beginning of November, six children were selected for more in-depth study in order to explore the unique ways individual children addressed the communicative challenges of their multilingual classroom.

I chunked episodes that followed a particular child through the months of the study. By comparing episodes from different times, I could trace some evolution of children's efforts to make sense of classroom talk and of kindergarten tasks. This was not a quantitative study that compared, for example, change in mean length of utterance over time. But selective comparison of episodes from different times in the study did yield information about changes in children's use of English, such as mastering new vocabulary and achieving more standard word order or more conventional use of pronouns. For example, Pierre's evolving mastery of the label *red* for the color red became obvious through comparison of episodes from different times relating to colors.

Through this comparative analysis, I could detect patterns in the communicative behaviors that case study children used to negotiate shared meanings with the teacher and with each other, and to interact in English in new situations with a wider circle of children. My use of the term *strategies* throughout this book refers to recurring patterns of behavior involved in efforts to accomplish communication-related goals. An example of one strategy is Pierre's and Gennady's enacting familiar superhero roles with associated verbal expressions (such as "Go, go, Power Rangers!") in order to support sustained interaction during play. Although the children's goals in their own minds might be social ones, the pattern of behavior served communicative goals as well.

After portrayals of the case study children were constructed, certain commonalities and contrasts emerged that related to the key communicative challenges for these L2 learners and their teacher in their multilingual classroom.

PLAN OF THE BOOK

Chapter 2 provides an overview of Mrs. Barker's ESL kindergarten. The large urban public school setting is described; the children, the teacher, and the program are introduced. Pierre and the other case study children are presented individually as communicators, socializers, and students.

Chapter 3 describes what efforts to establish intersubjectivity looked like and sounded like in the ESL kindergarten, especially early in the year. Establishing intersubjectivity was never simple. It involved much more than class members understanding literal meanings of each other's words— in itself a challenge—as teacher and children collaborated in establishing an understanding of the whys and how-tos of their classroom activities.

Chapter 4 illustrates the different ways that children's unique frames of reference for activities came to be more compatible with the teacher's goals. As children's expressive skills in English were developing, they often displayed characteristic ways of showing engagement with classroom events and activities. The teacher's inclination not to squelch but to legitimize these often very high profile behaviors fostered their evolution as valuable resources for language and literacy learning.

Chapter 5 describes the many ways children used teacher-provided regularities of schedule, activity formats, language patterns, and other teacher talk to support their participation in activities, their understanding of curriculum, and their English language learning. Nobody owned the words exclusively in Mrs. Barker's ESL kindergarten as she deliberately implemented strategies to make her English not only accessible but useful to her students. Some of the ways the children capitalized on her language were unanticipated by the teacher, as children appropriated her teacher talk for a combination of academic and social purposes.

Chapter 6 documents the many strategies for beginning to take ownership of English that were fueled by children's sociability—their eagerness to communicate and their efforts to cultivate friendships in informal contexts unmediated by the teacher. A collaborative model of peer scaffolding is introduced to account for the many occasions when children were on the giving or receiving end of peer support for L2 learning, enabling them to accomplish with each other what they could not originally do on their own.

Chapter 7 focuses on the case study child most unfamiliar with English and with school norms. He came into school eager to communicate his experiences, his preferences, and his intentions, but on his own terms and in his own language. The chapter traces how the teacher met the challenge of his different timetable for adapting to the ESL kindergarten by recognizing and nurturing his personal resources.

Chapter 8 reflects on the role of Mrs. Barker—her expectations, beliefs, skills, and compatible practices—in capitalizing on the resources she and the children brought to the challenges of making sense in their ESL kindergarten. The chapter provides a synthesizing perspective on the collaborative strategies used by the teacher and the children as they established links between social and academic purposes, between teacher-fronted and peer-mediated activities, and between language-learning strategies and ways of making sense of activities. Finally, the implications of this study for teachers, teacher educators, and researchers in multilingual early childhood settings are discussed.

Throughout this book, the case study children's efforts to make sense *in* and *of* the ESL kindergarten are revealed primarily through their voices and actions, as they engaged in curriculum activities and interacted with their peers and Mrs. Barker. The transcription conventions used are listed in the Appendix.

2

The ESL Kindergarten—
A Room for Talk

On Day 37, Jerry Yang comments with a wry grin on the budding relationship between Tracy Chen, a fellow Cantonese speaker, and Inga, their Russian-speaking tablemate.

JERRY: Him (pointing to Inga) *her* friend (pointing to Tracy). Him [Tracy] not *her* friend (pointing to Inga). Tomorrow, *both* friends. Inga *her* friend (points to Tracy). Tracy *her* friend (points to Inga).

Jerry had not sounded so philosophical a few weeks earlier when Inga first began experimenting with ways to insert herself into his frequent Snack Time Cantonese tête-à-têtes with Tracy, his close friend from prekindergarten. As he saw Tracy choosing Inga as a line partner several days in a row, he seemed rather jealous, and began to urge Inga: "Don't hold him fingers!" [Don't hold her hand!] However, by Day 13, Jerry also was experiencing some of the fun of the interactions in English across language backgrounds. Just after the teacher announced lunch that day, the three children collaborated in their first joke, based on a shared understanding of routines.

INGA: (lays her head on the table and pretends to sleep, periodically peering up at Jerry, smiling, and "going back to sleep")
JERRY: (grinning) Sleeping. Okay. Sleeping. Baby sleeping.
TRACY: (with a widening smile) Okay, sleep! No go lunch!
INGA: (as they all laugh and get in line) We're wonderful! Teacher, we're wonderful!

Inga's assertiveness in reaching across language backgrounds at her table mitigated against Tracy and Jerry's remaining an isolated Cantonese-speaking duo at her table, and was instrumental in Tracy's later announcement to speak "/aw/ English." Tracy, Jerry, and Inga are three of the six case study children who are the main focus of the book.

THE CLASS AS A WHOLE

The criterion of eligibility for Mrs. Barker's ESL kindergarten was performance below the 40th percentile on the Language Assessment Battery. Children with a home language other than English and children with Spanish surnames were automatically tested with the Language Assessment Battery.

Children's Language Backgrounds and Families

Of the 31 ELLs in the class, 16 were Cantonese Chinese speakers and 8 were Russian speakers. Among the remaining children, there were 2 Turkish speakers, 1 Fu Chow Chinese speaker, 1 Vietnamese speaker, 1 Albanian speaker, 1 Spanish speaker, and until late in the study, only 1 Haitian-Creole and French speaker. Kindergarten children had to have their fifth birthday during the calendar year in which the school session began.

Information about the children's lives outside of school was by and large unavailable to me. However, most of the Cantonese speakers had been born in the United States, whereas the families of the Russian-speaking children were more recent arrivals. Almost all the children in Mrs. Barker's class were neighborhood children, not "bus" children, although Pierre was an exception. At the end of the day, many were picked up by grandparents or by older siblings. Most of the children were eligible for the free-lunch program, and many of them lived as large extended families in small living quarters.

Many children in the class had close relatives in other classes. It was not uncommon for an older child to poke a head in the door of Mrs. Barker's classroom in the morning to explain why a sibling or cousin would be absent from Mrs. Barker's class that day.

Preferences of Chinese Parents

As I mentioned in Chapter 1, although the Chinese-speaking parents were offered a bilingual program for their children, they selected the ESL program. Moreover, they registered their children for school with English first names, not their Chinese first names. This was not a sign that the parents did not wish their children to be steeped in the home culture; many of the Chinese parents arranged for their children to attend Chinese school on the weekends. Some of the Chinese parents had specifically requested Mrs. Barker as a teacher for their current kindergarten children, based on the positive experiences of their older children or nieces and nephews in her classes of previous years.

The children sat in assigned seats and were grouped at tables of varying shapes and sizes accommodating 3 to 9 children. The seating arrangement and language backgrounds of the children are shown in Figure 2.1.

THE CASE STUDY CHILDREN

The three Cantonese-speaking case study children were Jerry, Tracy, and Robert. Since their English first names were used exclusively in school by the children themselves and by the teacher, English names are primarily used in this book. The miniportraits also include Chinese first and last names for each child. (All names in this book are pseudonyms.)

The two Russian-speaking case study children were Inga and Yakov. Pierre, the sixth case study child, was for much of the year the only student whose home language background was Haitian Creole and French. Jerry, Tracy, Inga, and Yakov were tablemates. Pierre and Robert sat at other tables.

The English proficiency among the case study children ranged from virtually none (Robert and Yakov) to limited (Jerry, Inga, Tracy, and Pierre). Inga was the most fluent English speaker of the six children when school began. All the children were highly reliant on paralinguistic cues, such as gestures and pantomime, and on visible referents, such as pictures and objects, to understand others' English and to supplement their own limited English expression. Their proficiency was limited in terms of grammatical construction, depth of vocabulary, and pronunciation.

As socializers, communicators, and students, the case study children each had characteristic ways of relating to the teacher, to peers, to curriculum, and to language choices at the beginning of the year.

Jerry

Jerry ("Jung-yi") Yang, 5 years and 3 months old when the term began, was not particularly tall, but often tried to establish himself as "bigger" among his peers. His broad forehead could suddenly furrow with dismay if someone claimed to be taller or to have a bigger Lego structure. When he was in prekindergarten across the hall the previous year, his older sis-

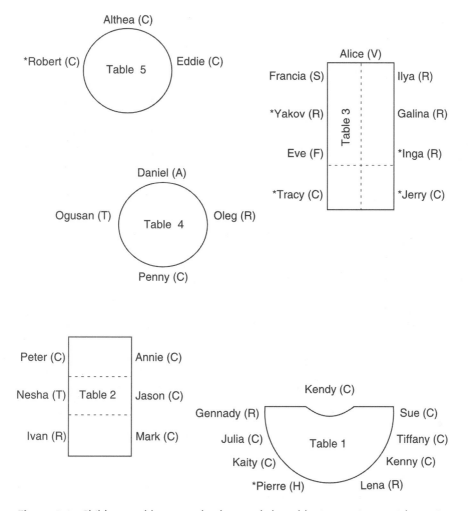

Figure 2.1. Children and language backgrounds by table. Letters in parentheses indicate language background: (A)—Albanian; (C)—Cantonese Chinese; (F)—Fu Chow Chinese; (H)—Haitian-Creole and French; (R)—Russian; (S)—Spanish; (T)—Turkish; (V)—Vietnamese. Asterisk indicates a case study child. Broken lines indicate several tables pushed together. At Table 3, Alice arrived in December 1993; also at Table 3, Eve departed midyear, and Janine (H) was transferred in and took her seat.

ter had been in Mrs. Barker's kindergarten. He came into kindergarten knowing a lot about letters and numbers, and enjoyed showing his peers how he could spell out all the name labels at his table. Jerry was much more inclined to display his knowledge at informal times among his peers than at Group Time with the teacher.

Jerry could often be found chatting in rapid Cantonese with many of his peers. However, from the first days of class, he was also very tuned into peer culture, and made great efforts to connect with children of other language backgrounds about certain popular peer symbols, such as sneaker symbols, in particular flashing LA Lights.

> JERRY: (pointing to Ogusan) What's her [his] name? What's her name?
> DANIEL: Her name? Her name is Ogusan.
> JERRY: (louder) Ogusan. Look at me. I got Lights!

Tracy

Tracy ("Ding-shi") Chen, at 5 years and 7 months, was one of the oldest students. Her delicate face, with its high cheekbones, often had a solemn look as she sat straight-backed at Group Time, gazing at Mrs. Barker. In contrast to Jerry, Tracy was very assertive in bidding for turns to show the teacher what she knew in Group Time activities. Although always mannerly with the teacher, she would use the weight of her parents' authority in disagreeing with her.

> T: You've still got your baby teeth, right? Big baby teeth.
> TRACY: No Teacher, my father say, I got *big* teeth!

Tracy entered kindergarten quite knowledgeable about print and was very proud of how quickly and neatly she wrote her letters. She would often write names of family members in her drawings. She talked about language itself, saying her brother Raymond's name was "so lots [long]."

Initially, Tracy used Cantonese predominantly in informal peer talk, but her use of English expanded as her friendship with Inga deepened. They used English for many purposes as they criticized each other's artwork, competed for the teacher's attention, clowned around, gossiped, expressed attitudes toward tasks, and asked for each other's help.

Tracy could be rather bossy in her play and often assigned other girls (except Inga) auxiliary roles as daughter or sister. Even as she spent more time with Inga, she was very loyal to Jerry, lashing out at children who criticized his artwork: "Don't say Jerry stink!"

Inga

Inga, five years and 2 months old, had light eyes and blondish brown hair pulled back in a ponytail. Her thin lips were notably expressive when she talked, and one cheek dimpled when she grinned. Inga had previously attended a private child care center. She had a brother in the third grade. Of all the case study children, Inga was the most colloquial speaker of English and seemed most accustomed to using it. She made up for a sparse vocabulary by her very adept use of pantomime and gesture. For instance, on Day 6, when a boy accidentally stepped on her construction paper, Inga picked it up and holding it in one hand, reported to Mrs. Barker: "When this fall (taps the paper with her free hand, he (points to the boy) stand (stamps her foot)."

Inga was assertive with teacher and peers alike. She seemed to identify very closely with the teacher, one day confiding to the teacher, "We two same eyes." When the teacher was losing in the board game Trouble because she couldn't get a double six on the dice, Inga boldly exclaimed, "What's wrong /wid/ you, I dunno!"

When Inga began kindergarten, she recognized very few letters of the alphabet and found writing a very laborious task. She was left-handed and tended to write from right to left, so that her name was written sequentially, but looked like mirror writing. This was a source of friction with Tracy, who couldn't resist flaunting her own competence.

Although Inga used English from the very beginning, she actually began to address Russian-speaking tablemates more often in Russian after the first few weeks of school. She was very aware that Yakov was using only Russian in school, and she would sometimes remark about it.

Yakov

Yakov, 5 years and 7 months old when the term began, was blonde, fair, tall, and slim. His vulnerable-looking mouth was more likely to grin than to break out in a full smile. As an only child who had not previously attended preschool, he seemed to have little experience cooperating with other children. Whether building with Legos or carefully creating a zoo habitat, he wanted complete control of the materials. The few English words that he used mostly carried a defensive message: "Mine! Stop! Don't touch!"

Yakov was the only child in the class to address everyone in his home language for the first several weeks of school. He came into kindergarten revealing the least knowledge of English of all the case study children. Only the most scripted games at Group Time engaged his attention. However, he eagerly addressed the teacher in Russian at more informal times for talk, evidently assuming she would be interested and would understand.

He had very little print knowledge when school began and showed no interest in either drawing or writing. Sitting at the same table as Inga, Tracy, and Jerry, he would spend most of his writing time trying to make a space for himself at the table and organizing his large box of crayons.

Pierre

Pierre, 5 years and 6 months old, was one of the tallest children in the class, but indicated that his family referred to him as "Petit Pierre" (Little Pierre). He had rich brown skin, and short, dark, tightly curled hair. He was bused in from another school in the district, and information was not available as to his place of birth and number of siblings. For much of the year, he was the only child in the class who spoke Haitian-Creole and French at home.

Pierre was very gregarious with the boys. His communication with his Russian- and Chinese-speaking tablemates consisted mostly of sound effects, high-energy mock fighting gestures, and stock English phrases from superhero scripts. Pierre tended to gather up steam in his play so that it often became somewhat giddy and very noisy; the teacher would some-times pull him up short with a "Pierre!" Pierre liked to savor funny moments and was appreciative of the antics of his peers, often urging them to "'fait' l'again!" [Do it again.] He often mixed French words in his English phrases.

Pierre was assertive in accessing the teacher at Group Time. For example, on Day 42, he checked in comfortably with the teacher about color labels.

> T: If you have yellow [a yellow math shape], put it in the box.
> PIERRE: 'Ça va' [Is this] yellow?
> T: You don't have yellow. You have orange.
> PIERRE: I got orange.

Pierre was assertive in making his needs known to the teacher during more informal times as well. As Snack Time approached, he would call across the room to the teacher, "Mrs. Barker, ma hungry!" Pierre was much admired for his very fine small motor coordination, which stood out during art and crafts projects. Very early in the year, he made a beautiful collage of a striding woman with black yarn Afro, blue cloth skirt, and big multicolored handbag. "'Ça ma' [That's my] mommy!" he announced.

Robert

Robert ("Luo-bo") Wu, at 5 years and 1 month old, was one of the younger children in the class, but was tall and sturdy. This was his first school experience and he also had a new baby sister at home. Robert had tearful difficulties separating from his mother each morning and would often lurk at the classroom doorway, hoping to catch a glimpse of her in the hall. All this may have been reflected in his play on Day 3.

> Robert places into a white box two white polar bears, one large and one small. Holding the big bear next to the small one, he says softly in English, "Baby," and makes kissing sounds. Then he lays several small bears down on their sides on the floor, and finally has the large bear lie down near them.

To ease Robert's adjustment, Mrs. Barker arranged for his mother to meet him during lunch on several days. His use of the word *baby* was one of the few English words I heard him speak early in the year.

At Play Time, Robert's interest in Legos and toy animals brought him in close proximity with some of the Russian-speaking boys, but he only talked to his Cantonese friends. His tablemates were Althea, who also had teary separations from her parents, and Eddie, who had attended prekindergarten the year before, but had seldom spoken, and never in English. However, Eddie showed by his actions that he understood academic tasks very well. Mrs. Barker felt early in the year that this was a companionable, socially supportive setup for all three children, and that Eddie would help Robert understand school tasks. Indeed, this seemed to be the case as Robert would often ask Eddie to display his knowledge of letters and numbers.

The only times Robert accessed the teacher early in the year were to ask, "Play?" He often remained at his table for at least part of Group Time. If he didn't quite understand how to do a task, he did not access the teacher. He would watch his tablemates and try to duplicate what they did.

By observing these individual children, I hoped to capture their different perspectives on meeting the challenges of getting into English, establishing intersubjectivity with their teacher and each other, and making sense of curriculum in their multilingual classroom.

THE SCHOOL

Mrs. Barker's ESL kindergarten (K-204) was part of a large school for children from prekindergarten (Pre-K) to Grade 5 in an imposing five-story gray brick building, which took up half of a square city block and had a very large fenced-in concrete schoolyard. Ceilings were high, walls ranged from a pale institutional gray to a softer blue, and the many "up" and "down" staircases were numbered and were bordered on their open side by a thin wire mesh. Through the windows in the stairwells, children could fleetingly glimpse narrow patches of concrete and sky.

The side corridor of the second floor constituted a separate wing, which housed, in addition to K-204, three other kindergartens, the school's pre-kindergarten, one 6–8-year-old special education class, and the main ESL office. One kindergarten, right next door to K-204, was the second ESL kindergarten, to which Mrs. Barker's children soon felt especially connected. The teacher, Mrs. Weinstein, was a very close colleague of Mrs. Barker and popped into the room frequently for brief consultations. In addition, Mrs. Barker's room had no bathroom, and Mrs. Weinstein generously allowed Mrs. Barker's children to enter her room in pairs at any time to use her bathroom.

THE CLASSROOM

Figure 2.2 shows the classroom layout. The meeting area at the front of the classroom was the one big stretch of empty vinyl-tiled floor space in a room bordered by closets and shelving, blackboards, and bulletin boards. The various shaped formica-topped tables and wooden chairs clustered together into groupings throughout the room, gobbled up the precious floor space directly in front of the block shelves and all around the book rack, which was laden front and back with casual piles of soft-covered picture books. The house corner—narrow, deep, and truly nestled into a corner—had room for several children to make use of the stove, sink, and refrigerator, the plastic tea set and pots, pans, muffin tins and artificial food packed away in the cabinets. There was room for children to put dolls in the crib, to feed "babies" in the high chair, to put friends in the carriage, to talk on the telephones, to ring up sales on the cash register, and to iron at the ironing board.

THE TEACHER

Mrs. Barker was a monolingual English speaker who had immigrated from the British Isles as an adult and had a British accent. Karen Barker had been teaching in this setting for 6 years, after 2 years of substitute teaching. Her undergraduate degree was in early childhood education and her graduate training was in TESOL (Teaching of English to Speakers of Other

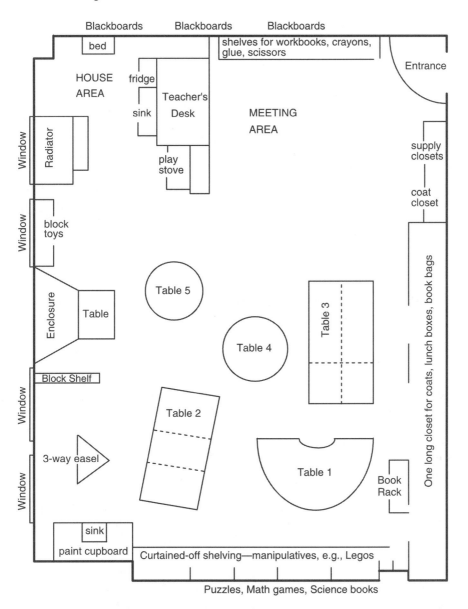

Figure 2.2. Classroom layout. Scale: 1 inch = 4 feet. Broken lines indicate several tables pushed together.

Languages). In this self-contained ESL kindergarten, Mrs. Barker's goals for language learning were integrated into content lessons and her language was tailored in specific ways to the needs of ELLs.

Mrs. Barker's respect for the linguistic and cultural diversity of children in her classroom was reflected in several ways. Although not steeped in any of the cultures, she was curious about them, particularly that of the group most numerously represented in her classroom, Chinese culture. She was in the midst of reading Amy Tan's *The Joy Luck Club* (1989) while this study was being conducted. She hoped it would give her some insight. She was keenly aware of parental expectations, and knew that the Chinese parents were particularly happy that she assigned daily homework. She was respectful of some families' preference not to celebrate birthdays or Halloween for religious reasons. She also knew that many of the Chinese-speaking children attended Chinese school on the weekends. Mrs. Barker considered children's home languages an asset. She felt that children's discussing concepts in their home language supported their understanding and learning.

The culture that Mrs. Barker most publicly celebrated was the Chinese one, especially around the time of the Chinese New Year. She involved the parents in this celebration; they brought platters of food for a festive luncheon. One father dressed up in a dragon costume and led the class in a dance all around their wing of the building. The festivities incorporated celebratory aspects of other cultures. For instance, one highlight of the Chinese New Year celebration was a piñata. As it turned out, the one Spanish-speaking child in the classroom put herself in charge of the plastic bat with which children were given turns to hit the piñata. The Chinese parents delightedly videotaped all aspects of the celebration.

In one sense, Mrs. Barker's integration of children's culture into the program was one of "food and holidays." But even on that level, it was not easy to provide experiences that the children would particularly appreciate as relating to them. For instance, Jerry did not like the "Cantonese cakes" the teacher made with the children for Chinese New Year. He explained to Inga and Tracy: "I don' like it delicious. I like eh candy, and bubble gum and juice and coke – – and water."

However, excerpts of children's talk that I had translated from Chinese indicated that the events and experiences did create an in-school context for active involvement with what Trueba (1981–82) termed the *dual context* of bilingualism, keeping children more closely connected with their culture. Sharing his Chinese New Year's joke with Tracy in Cantonese shows Jerry enjoying their "insider view" of their Chinese culture (translation in SMALL CAPS):

WHAT YEAR ARE YOU BORN IN? ARE YOU A DRAGON? ARE YOU BORN AS A
SNAKE? MONKEY? WHAT ARE YOU? TELL ME AND LATER I'LL TELL YOU. I'M A
DRAGON. WHAT ARE YOU? A HUMAN. HEEHEE, YOU'RE A HUMAN!

In the school as a whole, the presence of a multicultural, multilingual population was publicly acknowledged mainly through the morning
ritual of the Pledge of Allegiance carried over the public address system
and led by two children from an upper grade. The children's brief announcements before the pledge were made in English and in one of the
home languages of children in the school, often Russian or Chinese.

Mrs. Barker expressed concern many times during the year about how
"her children" fit into the wider system of homogeneous groupings in the
school. Even in the kindergarten, there were one or two so-called gifted
classes for children who scored highest on a standardized test. Children
designated as ELLs did not have an entree to that track. Mrs. Barker wor-
ried lest her students' lack of English fluency be interpreted by some administrators and teachers in the school as a lack of academic competence.
She often had to battle against a policy of slating her students automatically
for the lowest first grades. Mrs. Barker took special pride in getting her children into higher classes. This pride was balanced by a desire to ensure that
they would all have "nice" teachers who would make them feel comfortable and who would recognize the potential behind the accented English
and behind some children's reticence to speak out. Mrs. Barker tended to
keep tabs on how "her children" were doing in the upper grades.

Her Views on Communication and Individuality

Mrs. Barker believed that using any and all means and any and all languages would eventually lead to increased use of English. She allowed
children a wide latitude for ways of expressing themselves in peer interactions. At play, children shared an impromptu onomatopoeic language
as they staged growl-filled mock fights with wild animal figures or "traffic" conversations consisting entirely of beeps and screeching sirens to
accompany "road trips" with small cars and trucks. Nonverbal attempts to
initiate friendly interaction could be seen frequently in the early days of
school, such as when Yakov and Eve (a Fu Chow speaker) took turns playfully poking each other's heads gently.

Slapstick clowning around and teasing characterized the initial relationship between Ivan, a Russian speaker, and Mark, a Chinese speaker,
who found themselves for a week seated together at the little brown table
near the house corner. They held tidbits of food a little bit out of each

other's reach and made silly noises into my tape recorder. Within a week, their communication developed a serious reciprocity, as Ivan, the more eager English speaker, found out from the teacher when Mark could go to the bathroom. Mark lent Ivan his crayons to "fix" his homework, and Ivan let Mark know what else he should be coloring.

Children who shared a home language found out quickly that speaking to each other in their home language would elicit no negative feedback from the teacher. Even when children spoke Cantonese to each other during a Group Time when the rule was "listen and learn," a reprimand had to do with talking in general, not talking Cantonese. Mrs. Barker seemed able to deal with the fact that children's use of their home language sometimes made her the outsider. When she reprimanded Mark and Jason who were talking incessantly in Cantonese while children were offering words for the Alphabet Chart Letter of the Week, she merely warned, "You boys better be talking about the letter 'P!'"

This classroom had a balance of teacher-directed Group Time and more informal contexts for talk during Play Time and Table Activities, where children could shape their own interaction. Group Time activities were the part of the program that provided children maximum exposure to the English of the only native speaker, Mrs. Barker, and she worked hard to make that English and those activities accessible to the children. She established very clear boundaries between different social contexts for talk, and clearly defined the participation structures (Philips, 1972) that were consistently associated with different activities. *Participation structures* are the norms for participation in specific encounters, including, for instance, rules for gaining a turn to speak and for indicating one's attentiveness, and particular constraints on whether and when to introduce a new topic (Erickson & Shultz, 1981).

For instance, at Group Time, the children and the teacher were always in the meeting area, a large floor area at the front of the room. Group Time activities accounted for approximately one-third of the school day, although not all in one block of time. The teacher made explicit that at such times, the flow of talk was between teacher and children, rather than between peers.

In contrast, she explicitly referred to Table Activities and Play Time, as "their turn to talk," indicating that it was the children's turn to organize their own ways of interacting without direct mediation from the teacher. Art projects, math workbook pages, and writing practice were all tasks that were carried out individually at children's tables. When children sat at their tables, there was an interpersonal quality to all the activities right from the beginning of school. Peers literally rubbed elbows with each other, and their papers and workbooks virtually overlapped to some extent on the crowded work surfaces of their tables. In a relaxed social atmosphere, the materials and requirements of tasks served as a concrete shared focus of attention that facilitated negotiation of shared meaning. Children were encouraged and, indeed, often needed to share crayons, glue, and other art materials. So from the first week, one heard lots of "Gimme!" and "Wait!" and "This is mine?" among almost all the children. At Play Time, children were allowed to choose their own play partners, as well as their own activities, and to move around the room freely.

Mrs. Barker explicitly acknowledged that children do things at different rates. She made clear that those who hadn't finished snack could stay at their tables. Children saw each other being given different writing assignments, and seemed to develop a sense in this classroom that just because their friend had finished a task didn't mean that they had to rush to be done also.

Mrs. Barker tacitly acknowledged the individuality of her students in many ways. She allowed them to select their own particular entrée into using English in her classroom. For some, that might mean being high-profile responders at Group Time; for others, it might mean echoing a lot of the teacher's language; for still others, it might mean asking peers, "Is mine beautiful?" during art, or clowning around at Snack Time using gesture and laughter to supplement minimal English.

Her Views on Curriculum

Some of Mrs. Barker's broad goals were for her students to be comfortable in school, to become effective communicators in English, and to achieve a respect for, an understanding of, and an investment in school tasks. She incorporated very specific literacy-related goals into her program with an eye to preparing children for the Language Assessment Battery (LAB Test), their only gateway out of an ESL track in the future. Mrs. Barker acknowledged that not all the children were interested in writing letters and numbers, although many were. However, she was always conscious of the fact that knowledge of certain conventions of print and ability to recognize letters, numbers, and sight vocabulary were important to success on the LAB Test.

There were certain core whole-group activities that Mrs. Barker introduced in embryonic form right from the beginning of the year that continued to develop throughout the year. These activities were attendance; calendar; weather; seasonal and holiday songs and fingerplays; rote chanting of the alphabet and numbers; alphabet and number recognition quizzes; and creation of a class Alphabet Chart focusing on a Letter of the Week, featuring the letters in alphabetical order. The way that these developed over the year reflected Mrs. Barker's sense of curriculum as an incremental accumulation of knowledge over time. Sometimes Mrs. Barker articulated this sense, as, for example, on Day 24 when she said, "We've all learned 'A,' 'B,' 'C,' we've all learned '1' and '2,' we've all learned circle, we've all learned square, and we've all learned triangle. Today we're going to learn rectangle." As the children focused on new letters and numbers, the teacher gradually incorporated those into a recognition quiz; individual children would be called on to identify a number or letter pointed to by the teacher.

The gradual development of the core routines of attendance, calendar, and weather, which came to make up the Class News, also revealed Mrs. Barker's strategy of involving the children gradually in more and more aspects of an activity. Mrs. Barker, for example, modeled keeping track of the number of absent children each day by calling out "Absent one!" for the first child, "Absent two!" for the second child and keeping track on her fingers. Gradually more and more children took over this function. "Today we're going to learn what day it is. Today is Tuesday." Over a number of weeks, she added days of the week, the calendar day, the season, the month, the date, the year, and the weather. By December, these details about calendar and weather were part of Class News written on the board. The teacher began to involve the children in writing Class News by having them write in the date and draw a picture of the weather, both on the board and on a teacher-made monthly calendar. By mid-January, she was asking them how to spell some of the words. By February, children were volunteering to "read" the Class News with the teacher's pointer. Some copied Class News as their writing practice.

By the third week of school, the teacher introduced as part of the morning Group Time the Letter of the Week. She had a freestanding rack with chart paper that had solid and dotted lines indicating the height of upper and lower case letters. The first day of school each week, Mrs. Barker introduced a new letter. She wrote it in upper case and in lower case, and then had children come up to copy that along the top line. Then she asked children to think of words that began with that letter. When a child came up with a word, Mrs. Barker wrote it on the chart and that child got to come up and draw a picture representing the word. The Alphabet Chart was used again usually at least once or twice more during each week. Every time Mrs. Barker used the chart, she started with the *A* page, and had the children go over with her all the words so far.

As the year progressed, children participated in the Alphabet Chart activity in a variety of ways. Some actually could read the lists of words rhythmically along with the teacher; some echoed them; more and more children supplied new words for the chart; some children just repeated the new words. Some took wild guesses, as Mrs. Barker reassured, "It's okay to be wrong."

The potential dryness of the program was offset by Mrs. Barker's frequent introduction of interesting hands-on activities, her thrice daily read-alouds of children's books, and her allowing children the spontaneity to introduce topics from their own experience into some of the Group Time activities. For example, the Letter of the Week chart was both an activity about language and through language. Coupled with the predictability of the format, there was a spontaneity that stemmed from children being allowed to introduce their experiences from in and outside of the classroom through the words and phrases they contributed. Some suggestions, such as Robocop from the popular media, stimulated a lot of excited conversation.

Many of the activities during any particular week were thematically related and often many were anchored by the particular Letter of the Week. Mrs. Barker also used picture books frequently to introduce or enhance themes. Perhaps the most striking example of activities relating Letter of the Week to picture books to art activities to hands-on experiences occurred during *F* week. Mrs. Barker read the children *Jump, Frog, Jump!* (Kalan, 1989). Having discussed *whisper* and *secret* based on the story, she introduced a secret of her own by having them guess what she had in a brown bag. The secret was two large dead fish, which she passed around and discussed before they made fish prints. That same week, children made frog puppets. Mrs. Barker read *The Farmer in the Dell* (1988) and the children played the game. She introduced the big book *The Farmer and the Beet* (1989) and cooked beets with the children to make a dye for a different kind of printing. Language goals were integrated into all these classroom activities. For example, when Mrs. Barker reviewed *Jump, Frog, Jump!* she asked, "What came first? What came after the frog? What came next?" This sequencing language was becoming increasingly familiar to the children, as Mrs. Barker asked these same questions in relation to other books and activities.

Mrs. Barker methodically introduced new concepts each week, beginning with body parts, colors, and shapes early in the year. These provided additional regular opportunities to integrate concrete experiences, academic content, and language. She structured many different opportunities to handle materials and to use language related to the concepts. For example, in introducing the color blue, she started out by holding up a blue piece of paper. She pointed out and talked about all the blue in children's clothing, she sent children alone or in pairs around the room to "bring back something blue," and talked about the items as they accumulated in the middle of the circle. Finally, she had the children make collages with all different types of blue material. As the year progressed, Mrs. Barker explored with the children number concepts, size concepts, other math concepts, and concepts about opposites.

DAY IN THE SCHOOL YEAR	CALENDAR DATE
1	Sept. 20
11	Oct. 4
22	Oct. 20
29	Oct. 29
32	Nov. 3
37	Nov. 10
42	Nov. 17
46	Nov. 23
52	Dec. 3
55	Dec. 8
65	Dec. 22
67	Jan. 3
72	Jan. 10
77	Jan. 18
82	Jan. 25
90	Feb. 4
92	Feb. 8
99	Feb. 17
102	Mar. 1
112	Mar. 15
118	Mar. 23
130	Apr. 18

Figure 2.3. Calendar dates of selected school year days.

Returning to themes and to frequently used grammatical patterns, such as sequencing language, periodically during the year was a characteristic of Mrs. Barker's program, and one that gave children many chances to "tune in." The day of the school year is used to situate each event described in the time of the study. Figure 2.3 lists the calendar dates of selected school year days.

3

Establishing Intersubjectivity

In early spring, the children sit on the floor around Mrs. Barker as she shows them how to make a spring basket.

T: (as she folds and staples paper together into a basket) Now, Mrs. Barker will do this part for you.

INGA: Mrs. Barker gonna do that part for us. Cause that is *really* hard.

CHILD: A little basket to use trick or treat. (in high-pitched voice) Trick or treat! Trick or treat! . . .

INGA: (eyes widening suddenly) A basket! How you gonna *hold* it?

T: How am I gonna *hold* it? That's a great question.

INGA: (with a dimpled grin) Wha'? You gonna put it on your *head*? (as Mrs. Barker starts to assemble the handle from a strip of paper) You gonna make a circle like that and cut the circle and then you could hold it . . . I gonna make like Mrs. Barker . . . I know how we gonna make it. In that. It's gonna be like/ like a circle.

PIERRE: Li/li/ it's gonna be like a basket.

PETER: You *hold* it.

T: You *hold* it.

Moments later:

INGA: Wha' we gonna *do* /wid/ it?

T: You need candy (for the afternoon spring party).

I was observing the Group Time basket-making demonstration toward the end of the 6-month period I spent in Mrs. Barker's classroom. Group Time, when the children were gathered around the teacher in the meeting area, offered crucial opportunities for children's maximum exposure to the teacher's English; and a shared focus on here-and-now concrete referents such as the spring basket helped make classroom language and procedures understandable. But notice what an active part the children played in "making sense" of the language and of that activity. In the scene above, Mrs. Barker's, Inga's, and her classmates' talk was woven through the teacher's basket-making demonstration and transformed it into a forum for making sense on three different levels.

On the level of *literal* meanings, Inga, Pierre, Peter ("Bi-de") Cai, and others were making sense of the language itself, helping to showcase the meaning of key task-related vocabulary in this situation. They did this by contextualizing words such as *basket* and *hold* with, on the one hand, a familiar experience (Halloween trick-or-treating) and, on the other hand, a funny image (basket on the head) that helped convey the meaning of *hold* with comic relief. On this level of literal meanings, the weaving in and out of the children's language with the teacher's demonstration gave a chance for particular words to be associated with what the children were seeing.

In Mrs. Barker's class, this highlighting of literal meanings was often embedded in efforts to get at the *procedural* meaning, as children and Mrs. Barker clarified how to go about a task. Inga's question "How ya gonna *hold* it?" and her subsequent wisecrack "Wha'? You gonna put it on your *head*?" drew everyone's attention to a key element of the task, that is, making the handle.

On a third level of meaning, that of *relevance*, Inga and others wanted to know how this activity related to *them*: "A little basket to use trick or treat" and "Wha' we gonna *do* /wid/ it?" Weaving in that layer of meaning put the word *basket* into the familiar Halloween context, and that proved instrumental to Inga's understanding of the activity. Earlier that morning, when Mrs. Barker first mentioned they would be making "a spring basket to put your spring candy in," Inga's immediate response indicated that she did not understand the intended meaning of *spring basket*. She initially associated it with the piñata full of candy that they made for Chinese New Year, and she asked, "Then we're gonna hit it again?" So, for Inga herself, despite her seeming fluency, the meaning of *basket* was not clear until all three levels of meaning came together.

Six months into the school year, Mrs. Barker and the children constructed together a frame of reference in which not only the language but the hows and whys of the basket activity would make sense. As Dyson (1999) and Ballenger (1999) have pointed out, children bring their own frame of reference to curriculum activities, and it is important to know whether that frame of reference is compatible with the teacher's agenda. In Mrs. Barker's classroom, establishing intersubjectivity involved collaboration between teacher and children in making more compatible the often differing frames of reference they brought to curriculum events and activities. At this point in the year, Inga, Pierre, and Peter were able to articulate questions and statements that clarified the meaning of the basket demonstration. Their questions and comments seemed to flow without unusual effort and with an easy back-and-forth chiming in at Group Time.

Early in the school year, establishing intersubjectivity at Group Time did not involve such an easy flow of talk. At that earlier stage, Mrs. Barker used simple interactive games to implement the recommended L2 teaching strategy that "language has to be embedded in a context of gestures, demonstrations and activities that lead and support the learners' guesses about what is going on" (Wong Fillmore, 1982, p. 171). One example was a ball game at Group Time on Day 9.

> T: Let's make a circle.
> Child: We playing ball?
> T: When you throw the ball, say your name.

This was the third time in the first 2 weeks of school that the children were playing a name game with a ball at Group Time. They were beginning to use the predictable format (forming a circle) as a clue to the content of the activity. In different versions of this ball game, the child holding the ball had to say his or her name while rolling or throwing the ball to someone else. The predictable format and scripted participation carried with it minimum risk and encouraged children to take part.

INTERSUBJECTIVITY BETWEEN TEACHER AND GROUP

These interactive games represented one of an array of strategies Mrs. Barker employed to address a key challenge at the beginning of the school year: to establish and sustain a shared focus of attention with her class at Group Time. How would they know what she was talking about? How would she find out what they understood? How would they all know if they were all talking about the same thing? Meeting this challenge constituted what Wells (1981) has termed establishing *intersubjectivity*. Wells has pointed out that an essential process in meaningful communication between any two parties, in this case between peers or between teacher and student(s), requires the establishment of intersubjectivity. This is how he describes that process:

> Any act of linguistic communication involves the establishment of a triangular relationship between the sender, the receiver and the context or situation. The sender intends that, as a result of his communication, the receiver

should come to attend to the same situation as himself and construe it in the same way. For the communication to be successful, therefore, it is necessary (a) that the receiver should come to attend to the situation as intended by the sender; (b) that the sender should know that the receiver is so doing; and (c) that the receiver should know that the sender knows that this is the case. That is to say they need to establish intersubjectivity about the situation to which the communication refers. (p. 47)

To establish intersubjectivity at Group Time, Mrs. Barker used pantomime, gestures, facial expressions, props, blackboard drawings—anything to create a redundancy of clues as to the meaning of the language she employed. She picked here-and-now topics that were familiar to all the children, relating to body parts, colors, animals, and especially children's names, which she incorporated into a variety of interactive games.

Establishing Intersubjectivity: A Two-Way Street

The establishment of intersubjectivity was never really simple, nor was it limited to conveying literal meanings—even in those first few weeks during the ball games. Although all that the children needed to understand in order to participate was how to imitate the teacher and their peers in carrying out the predictable format and script of the game, some children "construed the situation" in a different way, bringing to the game their own frame of reference. Thus the children were not just working at receiving messages; they were sending some of their own, albeit nonverbal ones. They wanted to take some initiative and express their individual variation on "turning toward the topic" (Lindfors, 1999). For instance, the first time Mrs. Barker introduced the ball game, the children perked up visibly when Kendy introduced an innovation by bouncing the ball once before throwing it. Taking their cue from him, Mark and Oleg each bounced it twice when their turns came, and Gennady bounced it three times. Mrs. Barker did not respond to this behavior as "testing limits" or "seeing what they could get away with." Instead, she herself would join in and incorporate the variation into her own turn, much to the glee of the children. In this way, she conveyed the message that she could see the activity from the children's perspective, getting the joke and appreciating it. The children could see her "construing the situation" the same way they did and modifying how the game was played accordingly.

When children initiated such irreverent little variations, they were taking a risk that the teacher might not like it and would admonish them for fooling around. The fact that Mrs. Barker not only allowed the variation, but built on it herself, created an atmosphere in which children's idiosyncratic ways of turning toward a topic were welcome in her classroom.

Creating Insider Understandings

In the early days in this classroom, these small moments of shared humor were very precious and added spontaneity and lightness to the rather stilted adherence to a verbal script. Two different elements seemed to contribute to the lightness: an implicit mild irreverence toward "school rules" and the opportunity for children to shape in some very visible way encounters that were otherwise dominated by the teacher. The teacher herself sometimes took the lead in introducing these elements. One mildly irreverent joke that the teacher developed with the children was shared many times over the year. A shared appreciation of this joke depended on a shared perception of routines, in this case, the gap between the "ideal" and the "real" Rest Time.

During Mrs. Barker's reading of *Three Little Ducks* (Melser & Cowley, 1980) on the first day of school, when she got to the part where the ducks go to sleep, she said, "Everybody go to sleep," and had them pantomime with her "waking and stretching." She introduced this same exaggerated pantomime of waking and stretching at the end of the quiet time after lunch. As the weeks went by, the children all found this quite humorous because no one really slept during Rest Time. During one such Rest Time, Yakov pointed up the incongruity by pretending to snore loudly, and everyone chuckled including the teacher. By very late in the year, Rest Time had evolved into a time for quiet conversation while Mrs. Barker circulated among the tables and checked individual children's homework. Many children would still do a quickie version of the pantomime at the end of the period and grin at the teacher in a silent shared joke.

The whole class shared this kind of "insider understanding," based not so much on language as on shared perception of lived experience. Teacher and children made the same sense out of a recurring situation in the everyday life of the classroom. This built up a sense of solidarity in the classroom before there was widespread verbal participation in English during Group Time activities.

Early in the year, communication at Group Time was usually dominated by the teacher. Therefore, moments when she tried to establish a sense of collaboration for the children—to draw the children into shaping the outcome of an activity—stood out as very powerful. One such moment occurred when Mrs. Barker introduced a drawing and labeling game. "I'm going to draw the silliest picture you ever saw," she said, as she began to draw a person on the blackboard. As she added each body part, she would ask, "What am I making?" and the children were soon yelling out "eyes" "nose" and so on. But then she shifted her question from "What am I making?" to "What do I need now?" As the teacher stood with chalk poised near the blackboard, the children began to call out body parts or items of clothing that they wanted the teacher to add to the figures. Thus, with the same labeling vocabulary, the children were able to experience a more active role in shaping the activity. The children's role in shaping the activity was further reinforced by the teacher's accepting a change of topic. For example, when Pierre suggested "a car" in responding to a "What else should I draw" question, Mrs. Barker accepted the change of topic and drew one. Children's sense that this activity was an active collaboration between themselves and the teacher was expressed by the exclamation of one child to another teacher who walked into the room, momentarily interrupting the activity midstream: "Look what *we* did!"

Monitoring the Children's Perspective

Mrs. Barker's collaborating with the children in irreverent jokes was clear evidence of her willingness to see the activities from their perspective. Much later in the year, in early January, this sensitivity to how children were "construing the situation," to use Wells's (1981) terminology, very much contributed to maintaining intersubjectivity in more academic situations, such as in this whole-group math activity centering on the concept of "How many more?"

In this lesson, the teacher and the children sat in a circular formation on the floor, and she used the center of the circle to set up and solve problems with math manipulatives. Mrs. Barker would line up two sets of counters—each set different in shape and/or color—and ask first, "Which [group or set] is more?" and second, "How many more?" Then she would have one of the children match up the members of the sets, leaving the remainder from one of them, as in the following excerpt.

> T: (counting) One, two red shapes. Three red shapes. (T lines up three identical flat red hexagons.) One, two, three, let's see one, two, three, four, five blocks. (lines up five natural wood cubes) Which one is more?
> CHILD: Five.
> CHILDREN: Fi::ve.
> T: Five is more than three. How many more?
> INGA: Two.
> T: Two more. Come and do it.

As the teacher continued to set up problems of this type, the children became more vocal during the process and began to anticipate her questions. When Mrs. Barker started to lay out a set of bunny counters, the children joined in with her in counting them.

> T: One,   two, three, four, five, six. ⎤
> CHILDREN: Two, three, four, five, six. ⎦
> JULIA: Six rabbits.

Then Mrs. Barker began counting out the other shaped counter and received several different answers to her first question:

> T: One, two, three (puts out three of another shaped counter).
>   Which is more?
> CHILDREN: Three::::. ⎤
> PIERRE: Rabbits.   ⎦
> CHILD: Six.

On the face of it, several children seemed to be getting the wrong answer. The teacher then seemed to be figuring out why many children were saying "three," and realized that some were anticipating her second question. She reassured them, "I understand what you're doing."

> T: Which first? Give me no/ give me the answer first. *I understand
>   what you're doing. Six is more than three.* Rabbits is more. How
>   many more?
> T: Three more. Althea, come and do it. (Althea matches up three
>   of the rabbits with the three shapes in the other set.) How
>   many more rabbits?
> CHILDREN: Three.

This was a real example of what Wells refers to as the *triangular relationship* between sender (the teacher), receiver (the children), and context (the math problem). The children were being reassured that the teacher knew that they were not only "attending to the same situation," but that they understood the concept, that is, "construed the situation in the same way."

INTERSUBJECTIVITY BETWEEN TEACHER AND CHILD

There were many instances early in the year when teacher and children were not so sure what each other meant. In the many opportunities for one-to-one communication between Mrs. Barker and individual children, getting each other to "construe the situation in the same way" required much effort from both parties, and the efforts did not always meet with unqualified success. It was very clear in one-to-one interactions between Mrs. Barker and individual children that both teacher and child collaborated actively in implementing multiple strategies for clarifying each other's meanings. The need for multiple strategies in establishing intersubjectivity, and the collaborative nature of the efforts, were very evident in many of these day-to-day interactions. Even reliance on shared concrete referents such as task-related materials, toys, and food did not in themselves guarantee successful negotiation of shared meanings. I turn now to interactions between Mrs. Barker and each of two case study children, Tracy and Yakov, to clarify the kinds of issues that arose in their efforts to understand each other early in the year.

Negotiating Meanings with Concrete Cues

Many of Tracy's early interactions with the teacher were focused on tasks; sometimes, because the topic was very concrete, Mrs. Barker could use a "show me" strategy rather than depending primarily on language. Here is one example:

> TRACY: (working on her dog puppet) Red glue, Teacher? Red glue?
> T: Glue with a red top you mean?
> TRACY: Red glue.
> T: Which glue? Show me.
> TRACY: Show you. (They go to the shelf.) Blue glue [with a blue top].
> T: Blue glue. Not red glue. Annie has the blue glue.

Even this relatively simple set of interchanges involved a kind of collaboration between teacher and child, where each followed the other's lead, and where the teacher suggested the strategy that clinched the establishment of intersubjectivity. There were other situations where Tracy took the lead in introducing a different strategy to reach understanding. In the following episode, again revolving around glue, Tracy took the initiative in rephrasing the teacher's directive to check the meaning.

> TRACY: Teacher, look. No more glue in here.
> T: Use a different glue.
> TRACY: Teacher, no more glue.
> T: Use a different glue.
> TRACY: Teacher, other one glue?
> T: Yes please, different one. (Tracy goes and gets another.)

Negotiating Without Here-and-Now Cues

Although concrete referents played a crucial role in teacher-child interactions focused on the here-and-now of classroom life, they were not much help when the topic of conversation focused on aspects of lives outside of school. As the year progressed, children wanted more and more to be able to draw on their own experiences in responding to stories at Group Time and to chat with the teacher about aspects of their lives outside of school. Tracy, in particular, often without preamble would start to talk to the teacher about a topic from the "there-and-then" of home and family. On such occasions, it was much harder for her to establish intersubjectivity with the teacher; and even with a lot of patience and effort on both their parts, they sometimes only achieved partial understanding. It is clear that they were both working very hard in the following episode.

> During the Dog Puppet activity on Day 25, Tracy begins by talking about her brother, and then suddenly switches to conveying a question from her mother about Mrs. Barker's babies. Tracy's use of the pronoun *you* for *he, your,* and *they* contributes to the teacher's difficulty in understanding her. Tracy's strategies are to repeat herself and later on to emphasize certain words more. The teacher's strategies are to repeat or rephrase Tracy's messages in question form to confirm her guess as to Tracy's meanings.

TRACY: Teacher, Teacher, you remember, my bludder [brother] you like orange.

T: You like orange?

TRACY: My bludder a like mine.

T: My brother? Brother?

TRACY: My bludder you like orange.

T: He likes orange only? Doesn't he like other colors too? Just orange? Does he like red?

TRACY: No. My momma tell my say/ say your baby how are you, you two. You two baby, how are you?

T: There's two?

TRACY: You two baby. How are you?

T: How are you?

TRACY: How are you, you two baby?

T: How old are you, that question?

TRACY: No. How *are* you, you *baby*?

T: How old is my baby? Oh *my* baby, not *her* baby. *My* baby, I gotta baby who's zero. She's only 2 months. She's not one yet. Three

months, sorry. Three months. And I've got a baby who's
3 years old. I got two little girls. Rebecca and Emily. Momma
wanted to know?
TRACY: My momma tell my.
T: Okay.

It seemed to me after listening to this episode many times on the
audiotape for transcription, that Tracy was asking on behalf of her mother
how Mrs. Barker's two babies were. That was not the conclusion that Mrs.
Barker reached at the end of this sustained set of interchanges. But Tracy
seemed somewhat satisfied. What made it harder for the teacher with some
of the children, including Tracy, was the fact that their pronunciation of
English words was very strongly colored by the sound system of their own
first language. This sometimes made it hard to understand their words
without hearing them several times. Thus, in order to be able to appreciate fully a child's message and achieve intersubjectivity, the teacher needed
to be very familiar with any particular child's speech.

Because I had to transcribe from audiotapes the speech that I heard,
I had greater exposure to the children's pronunciation and speech patterns
than the teacher did. This sometimes led to my interpreting a child's English word for the teacher. I played such a role later in the year in the following episode, one that illustrates how just a single word in a whole set
of interchanges could be absolutely crucial to making sense of the whole
narrative. The reader will notice that in comparison to the interaction about
the "two babies" in October, Tracy has in January used the correct pronouns and some past tense markers. Her story also does not come out of
the blue, but is very related to the story the teacher has been reading.
Yet because of the pronunciation of one word, *watch,* the story is hard to
understand.

After the winter break (Day 72), Mrs. Barker has been reading the
big book *Here It's Winter* (Beal, 1991) at Group Time, and talking
about how ice is slippery and how a man slipped on the ice. Tracy,
contributing to the emerging class trend of introducing narratives
during morning Group Time, offers a narrative, which is finally
understood by the teacher:

TRACY: My father is soon go to my Grampa's and he was // falling
    down, but my mother say "Look, watch." [She pronounces it
    more like /wash/.]
T: Sh sh. Look what?
TRACY: He *watch,* she say/ mother say

T: He was rushing?
TRACY: Father's falling down ⎤
RES: (to T) She said watch. ⎦ *Watch.*
T: (to Tracy) Wa::tch.
TRACY: (to T) Watch and he said/ he said and he not falling down.
T: He did not fall down because he watched? There you go!

It turned out that I was not the only resident "expert" on children's accents. The children themselves, because they had opportunities to talk to each other often during the day, were also able to serve as interpreters for each other with the teacher. For example, in January, Tracy offered a new word for the *B* page of the Alphabet Chart they used during morning Group Time. The word sounded like "/bukli/," and although she repeated it several times, it did not become clear what she meant. Only Inga, who as Tracy's best friend had much exposure to her English, was able to discern that Tracy was trying to say "Brooklyn."

Tracy began to develop other strategies for negotiating shared meaning when her pronunciation made her meaning unclear to Mrs. Barker. In negotiations that revolved around words she offered for the Alphabet Chart, the focus of attention was language itself. In one such instance, Tracy used pantomime and also offered a functional definition of a word.

TRACY: How about /frok/?
T: Frog?
TRACY: No. Ead da food. (She pantomimes eating with a fork.)
T: Fork? That's F.

Negotiating Without a Common Language

In Tracy's negotiation of shared meaning with the teacher, the struggle was always over what Tracy or the teacher meant in English. When verbal interaction between teacher and a child took place without a common language, negotiation depended more exclusively and crucially on referral to visible cues, such as concrete objects, facial expressions, and physical gestures. In this kindergarten, Yakov was the only child who persisted in using his home language (Russian) in his one-to-one interactions with the teacher during the first several weeks of school. His persistence in doing so seemed to reflect his trust that the adults not only would welcome his talk, but would also divine his meaning—even if they always replied either in English or with an encouraging nod and smile.

In some situations, such as at Snack Time on Day 7, it was indeed easy for the teacher to guess his meaning and to respond appropriately. When

Yakov approached Mrs. Barker, held up his empty drink box, patted his stomach, and said something in Russian, Mrs. Barker replied, "In your tummy?" Yakov's gestures and the concrete visible referent—a drink box, coupled with the fact that it was Snack Time—provided enough clues so that Yakov and Mrs. Barker could both feel confident that they were talking about the same thing. Engaging in *dilingual discourse* (Saville-Troike, 1987), in which each used a different language, did not prevent them from establishing that sense of shared focus, or intersubjectivity.

There were, however, situations in which even paying attention to Yakov's gestures and referring to concrete objects did not guarantee avoidance of serious misunderstandings. During Play Time on that very same day, Mrs. Barker caught Yakov putting school toys into his bookbag and reprimanded him angrily. Yakov, in great distress, retreated to the wall near the blackboard and knelt down facing it. His eyes glistened with barely contained tears, and his cheeks burned with bright circular patches of red. When the teacher saw his display of intense humiliation, it soon dawned upon her that he may indeed have asked her permission in Russian to take the toys home. She may have interpreted his combination of Russian and gestures toward the toy shelf as a request for permission to play with the toys, and answered with a smile and an encouraging nod. Mrs. Barker decided to explain to his mother what had happened.

Soon after this painful episode, on Day 17, Yakov began to orchestrate brief, frequent encounters for negotiating shared meanings with Mrs. Barker in English. In these interactions during drawing and writing activities at his table, he often used a crayon as a concrete visible referent that served as a clear, shared focus between himself and Mrs. Barker. Yakov would say "Look!" to get the teacher's attention and would then wait for her to provide the English name for the color of the crayon in his hand, or to confirm that he had named it correctly. This reached a peak of eight times in 15 minutes on Day 25, after Yakov brought in from home a special pack of 64 crayons. Mrs. Barker always made herself accessible and would respond within a moment or two.

Yakov, in initiating these encounters with Mrs. Barker, seemed to be creating a safe space for interacting with the teacher, structuring an unambiguous situation in which his intentions would not be misunderstood. During that same period, he did not stop frequent use of Russian in his interactions with the teacher. However, in the "crayon" interactions, he was structuring opportunities for himself to try out methodically what were for him new strategies for negotiating shared meanings in English, the strategy of requesting an English label for an object and the strategy of a confirmation check on his own use of a label.

WELCOMING CHILDREN'S PERSONAL STRATEGIES

Mrs. Barker accommodated Yakov's earliest efforts to establish intersubjectivity in English by allowing him to select and structure the situation through which he would first get into English. This was just one example of her appreciation for a child's perspective and her openness to allowing children's actions and voices to influence the shaping of activities and interactions with her. Her response was consistent with her acknowledging children's perspectives on how the ball games should be played in the early efforts to establish intersubjectivity between teacher and group. In the same spirit as her response to Yakov, Mrs. Barker gave Inga's and Pierre's distinctive personal strategies for making sense of activities a legitimate role in their engagement with the kindergarten curriculum.

4

Ways of Turning Toward the Topic

On Day 72, Mrs. Barker is demonstrating how to string a necklace of styrofoam shapes, bows, and tissue paper in an activity for N, the Letter of the Week.

T: (holding up a large, plastic, blunt-ended needle) Here we have a needle.
CHILDREN: Needle.
T: And it's made of plastic. This isn't sharp, see? . . . But do you touch anybody with this?
CHILDREN: No.
T: Or you won't make your – – – necklace.
INGA: We're gonna make a necklace? . . . It's gonna be *us* necklace or *mother* necklace?

. . .

INGA: I'm gonna make it beautiful like Teacher because Teacher's gonna show us how to do it, right?

INGA'S QUESTIONING

By this time in the year, I had come to expect Inga to ask questions about the purpose and relevance of the tasks the teacher demonstrated at Group Time. Lindfors (1999) states that "children inquire in somewhat predictable expressive ways that confirm our expectations . . . or that surprise us" (p. 185). As early as Day 6, Inga began to initiate interaction with Mrs. Barker about the practical details of tasks. "What do we have to *do*?" Inga asked, as the teacher started to demonstrate making head and shoulder portraits with collage and crayons. As Inga continued to initiate such interactions over time, I experienced a sense of déjà vu—of having seen that approach to similar events before. On Day 13, she pursed her lips as she studied Mrs. Barker's scanty sample of "blue, brown, and black" collage taped to the blackboard. "Teacher, we have to make this?" she asked. As the year progressed, Inga's questions became increasingly specific as to purpose. When they were making Halloween hats on Day 29, she wanted to know just what they would do with them: "We gonna take it in a party? Yeah?" Pointing at Mrs. Barker's completed hat, she queried further, "Teacher, we're gonna *go* with this?" Mrs. Barker responded, "Everybody's gonna wear their hats all day." On Day 118, during the basket-making demonstration described in Chapter 3, Inga could still be relied upon to come up with practical questions about the task and to inquire, "Wha' we gonna *do* /wid/ it?"

A Stable-Across-Contexts Style

Inga's characteristic pattern of inquiry in these situations was a part of what Lindfors (1999) has termed her *distinctive inquiry self*. Lindfors goes on to elaborate that for each child, there is "a unique profile, a stable-self-across-contexts style that is a set of expected tendencies, orientation, stance, preferred language-and-action ways of relating to phenomena of interest and of engaging others in his sense-making" (p. 190).

Inga's characteristic pattern of inquiry could be considered "stable across contexts" because she exhibited it not only during many art demonstration–related events over time, but because her interest in the how and why of activities later focused also on more traditionally academic literacy-related activities. For instance, during morning Group Time on Day 116, Inga expressed curiosity about the teacher's use of symbols on the lunch form.

> The children are watching Mrs. Barker fill in the lunch form after taking attendance when Ogusan initiates the questioning and Inga quickly pushes for more detail.
>
> OGUSAN: (to T) What are you doing like that?
> T: (to Ogusan) It's just the lunch thing // who's in school to have lunch.
> INGA: (to T) The A's is somebody not at school?
> T: (to Inga) Right. A for absent.
> INGA: (to T) And if it's a 'Yes' so it's good. It's not absent.

Inga's persistent questioning came to be recognizable as an expected tendency; her *orientation* toward teacher demonstrations was to figure out their procedures and the activities' relevance to her. Moreover, she adopted an assertive, questioning *stance* toward the teacher, sometimes with a wise-cracking edge to it, as in the basket-making demonstration.

Language-and-Action Ways

Lindfors(1999) refers to children's styles of inquiry—of making sense of events and activities—not just as ways with language, but as "language-and-action" ways because children's talk is embedded in their activities. When they are "doing" activities, the expectations for how they "do" them—both in terms of language and other behaviors—are somewhat shaped by the activity they are engaged in. For example, Mrs. Barker's kindergarten students were expected to "listen and learn" as a way to show their engagement in the teacher's Group Time demonstrations. The particular ways in which individual children acted out their engagement varied considerably. Some children sat quietly watching. Inga acted out her engagement by initiating persistent interactions with the teacher in order to negotiate meanings through her questions. Pierre acted out his engagement in many Group Time activities by treating them as dramatic events in which he became a performer. Inga's and Pierre's communications at these times were language-and-action ways—inextricably bound up in their actions showing engagement, in their orientation toward the activity, and in their stance toward the teacher.

Lindfors focused on children's sets of expected tendencies with regard to pursuing inquiry. She points out that Dyson's case study research (1989) on young children's development as writers employed a similar construct in describing "their individual styles as symbolizers and socializers," and each individual writer's "approaches" and "preferred ways of responding" (Dyson, quoted in Lindfors, 1999, p. 188).

In this chapter, Lindfors's (1999) notion of a unique profile is used to describe the distinctive blends of personal resources—the recurring expressive tendencies—that Inga and Pierre brought to bear in making sense of particular events and activities. The evolution of their preferred language-and-action ways of relating to these events and activities and to Mrs. Barker is traced and the impact on their engagement with language and literacy curriculum is described.

INGA'S LANGUAGE-AND-ACTION WAYS

In addition to her persistent questioning about the why and how of activities, Inga exhibited two other stable-across-context tendencies in her efforts to make sense of her ESL kindergarten. She often tried to see events happening around her through the teacher's perspective, tuning in, as it were, to the "big picture." She also enjoyed creating scenarios through a combination of speech and pantomime. She often used such scenarios as a way to react to selected events in the classroom by acting out their imagined consequences.

Tuning into the Big Picture

Inga seemed able to decenter—to put herself in the teacher's shoes—when she considered classroom events. For instance, on Day 102 (in March), when she saw me watching her tablemate Ilya sitting downcast during Rest Time–Homework Check, she volunteered that the teacher was very angry at him because he did "something bad." Then when she heard the teacher praise him for his homework, she looked up and remarked, "Now Mrs. Barker is happy for him."

Further evidence that Inga was tuned into the big picture from the teacher's perspective came from her interchange with Jerry on Day 113. The children were making clocks with movable hands from their math workbooks. Jerry wondered aloud why Tiffany was making a clock, since the teacher had already used Tiffany's clock materials in making the demonstration model. Inga explained: "She's [Tiffany's] making it for *Gennady*. Because Gennady is absent and Mrs. Barker make *hers* [Tiffany's]."

Inga sometimes expressed her understanding of the teacher's perspective by creating and acting out a short scenario in pantomime and dialogue. For instance, she created a scenario to reveal the teacher's perspective on why it was important for children to write their names on their spring baskets. "We gotta [write our name]. Cause she know/ she not gonna know. (She pretends to be the teacher asking whose work she has, pantomiming holding up papers for children to see.) Who is dis? Who is dis?"

Creating Scenarios

In the above scenario, Inga was able to express an understanding of cause and effect through playing out the consequences of an imagined event. Her use of a combination of language and pantomime to create such scenarios emerged as a stable-across-contexts style of reacting to ideas that struck her as having particular logical consequences, some of them quite funny or absurd. On Day 110, she enlisted Jerry and Ilya to collaborate with her in a stunningly clear scenario, in which Inga imagined herself literally in the teacher's shoes.

It is Mrs. Barker's birthday, and she has received fresh flowers for the occasion. She puts them with their wrapping into a bucket of fresh water and leaves them by the sink. Several children begin to say that the flowers are growing. At that point, Inga stands up and says to Jerry, "It's gonna grow up to the sky, up to the sky like this," and she raises her hand high. "Mrs. Barker is gonna bring it into the house like this," continues Inga with a grin, as she stretches her arms forward and, looking up at the imaginary blossoms, takes several halting steps, leaning back a little as if balancing a tall ungainly plant. As she finishes this pantomime, Jerry jumps up and says, "It's gonna be like this." He stretches his arms out to his sides as wide as they will go, then joins hands with Inga who is stretching hers wide. Then Inga says to Ilya on her other side, "And Ilya, like this." She grabs his hand and the three children stretch out to make one long span. By this time, the whole class is enjoying the scene.

For the teacher, witnessing Inga in this type of enactment provided a window into her way of thinking. For her classmates, Inga's ability to conjure up a dramatic scenario and make it visible to everyone through her expressive pantomime was valuable in establishing enjoyable moments of intersubjectivity. For Inga, enacting these scenarios provided experience in constructing imaginative English narratives through a combination of visual and verbal imagery.

Integrating Language-and-Action Ways

In the above scenario, Inga's ability to play out imagined consequences was very visible. The combination of Inga's language-and-action ways of making sense in her classroom world turned out to be a perfect fit for getting the most out of some of the language comprehension workbook activities. Inga's assertiveness with the teacher, her drive to get at the purpose of a task, her interest in the teacher's perspective, her penchant to create dramatic scenarios with dialogue, and her increasing interest in literacy conventions all came together in her response to a Group Time language comprehension workbook activity on Day 118.

The children, workbooks in hand, are seated in a circle in the meeting area. For each exercise set, there are six rows of pictures. The first row introduces a series of three pictures, each depicting people in a different home or school-like scene assumed to be familiar to children (for example, a child going to the playground, a child walking to the blackboard, and a child sitting at a classroom desk). The same picture series is repeated in Rows 2 and 3. The fourth row introduces a new series of pictures which is repeated in Rows 5 and 6. Children put their finger on the row called by the teacher, and after she presents a one-sentence descriptive scenario, they have to circle the picture that best fits that scenario. Mrs. Barker creates scenarios such as "'Please Mrs. Barker,' says the little girl, 'May I go outside to play?'" Then she directs, "Circle the one where the children go outside to play." By the time they reach the end of the second exercise set, Inga is beginning to make up her own scenarios to fit the pictures.

INGA: Band-Aid. Please, Mrs. Barker, may I have a Band-Aid? ⎤
T: (to class) Put your finger on number six. ⎦
INGA: May I have a Band-Aid?
T: (to class, creating her scenario) Mrs. Barker, I hurt my elbow. May I go to the nurse and get a Band-Aid?

A little later, they come to three rows depicting people in the living room, bathroom, and kitchen respectively. The teacher describes a different scenario for each of Rows 4 and 5. Inga, by the process of elimination, is predicting the answer to Row 6 before Mrs. Barker gets to it.

INGA: Cooking. Cooking. Cooking it's gonna be. Number six is cooking.
T: Well, the powers of deduction are at work in Inga's corner. Put your finger on number 6.
INGA: Cooking, cooking.
T: I like to cook in my kitchen. Number 6. I like to cook in my kitchen.

In this episode, the teacher did not react to Inga with annoyance at giving the answer away or answering out of turn. Instead, she explicitly recognized Inga's response as a sign of her logical thinking, acknowledging her "powers of deduction." Giving Inga this kind of space to react made room for the mastery that she achieved and displayed. She showed that she understood the big picture, the structure of the activity not just from the student's point of view—choosing what picture fit the scenario—but also from the teacher's point of view—making up the scenario and seeing each set of three rows of pictures as a whole unit.

By again imagining herself in the teacher's shoes in an academic activity, Inga transformed what started as a rather dry activity for receptive skills into a more engaging forum for using expressive language skills as st to the scenarios in which Inga's language was linked most own pantomime, during the workbook activity Inga's lane the narrative "text" to accompany printed pictures.

PIERRE'S LANGUAGE-AND-ACTION WAYS

Like Inga, Pierre also had a set of "preferred language-and-action ways of relating to phenomena of interest and of engaging others in his sense-making" (Lindfors, 1999, p. 190). This was most striking from very early in the school year during two types of teacher-orchestrated Group Time activities: Mrs. Barker's read-alouds and her demonstrations of how to make puppets for the Letter of the Week. Pierre treated the read-alouds and the puppet-making demonstrations as dramatic events, and he would respond by adding new dimensions to the teacher's performance. Pierre's early contributions to these dramatic events took the form of pantomime and sound effects that clearly matched the meanings the teacher was trying to convey.

Performing the Meaning of Texts

Pierre's tendency to treat Group Time activities as dramatic events was first evident during a read-aloud in the meeting area on Day 16, when he began to accompany the teacher's reading of the text with sound effects.

> Pierre sits with his long legs crossed and listens wide-eyed, his head tilted up and to one side as Mrs. Barker begins reading *What Comes in 2's, 3's, & 4's* (Aker, 1990). During the story-reading, as Mrs. Barker names and points to two eyes, or two arms, or two pieces of bread in the book, she interjects a predictable rhythmic counting "one, two," and children start to chime in. But when Mrs. Barker mentions airplanes, Pierre starts to respond with sound effects that showcase the meaning otherwise conveyed by word and picture.
>
> T: "Birds have two wings." One, two. "And so do airplanes."
> PIERRE: (drones like an airplane)
> T: One, two ". . . Traffic signals have three lights. Red for stop, yellow
>   for slow, and green for go." One, two, three. (points at each)
> OGUSAN: What is this? See i' says go?
> T: It says slow down. Slow down. Green is go.
> PIERRE: (makes sound of squealing brakes)
> . . .
> T: Yellow is slow::::: down. Green says go.

PIERRE: (warming to his role, starts to hum like a motor)
T: (in a warning tone) Pierre! (He stops.)
. . .
T: "The chair has four legs and so does the table."
. . .
T: "So does the cat."
T: One, two, three, four.   ⎤
CHILDREN: One, two, three, four.   ⎥
PIERRE: Mee-ow:::   ⎦

Pierre's mode of constructing meaning in this example through acting out the read-aloud is characteristic of young native English speakers (Hickman, 1983; Kiefer, 1986) and ELLs (Fassler, 1998), and certainly would be considered appropriate behavior if he were looking at the book on his own. At Group Time, however, his responding with action and sound effects might receive a questionable reception from the teacher, as it might be seen as potentially distracting from the teacher's reading. Indeed, Mrs. Barker did not seem altogether thrilled by Pierre's irrepressible responses on Day 16. However, she was unequivocally accepting when he responded with an even more active performance on Day 25, during her demonstration of how to make a dog puppet for D, the Letter of the Week. Mrs. Barker actually took a cue from Pierre and incorporated pantomime into her own presentation. Pierre and the teacher, as partners in improvisation, produced moments of synchronized coperformance that delighted the class and highlighted the teacher's meanings.

> Mrs. Barker holds up a ditto sheet of an animal, which several children identify as a dog. When Mrs. Barker counters with, "It's a do::g? How do you know?" Pierre responds, "He's real hungry, you see." Pierre gets up on his knees, sticks his tongue out, and begins panting and then barking. In so doing, he deftly captures the stance and implied action of the dog in the picture, and Mrs. Barker immediately appropriates part of Pierre's performance for her continued discussion with the children.

T: He's hungry. He's going (T sticks out tongue and pants). What's that? (points at dog's tongue)
CHILD: Tongue.
T: Tongue? What's that? (points at dog's nose)
SEVERAL CHILDREN: Nose.
T: Nose. Dogs go (T sniffs) with their noses.
PIERRE: Woof, woof. (high-pitched)

While Mrs. Barker elaborates instructions in the demonstration, Pierre sometimes responds with barking and at other times spouts back the teacher's words; at one point, Pierre and Mrs. Barker synchronize their acts.

> T: Well, the first thing I have to do is color my dog, make my dog look beautiful. What color dog do I have?
> CHILD: Brown.
> T: Brown dog?
> PIERRE: Brown dog.
> . . .
> T: (makes her puppet move) ⎤
> PIERRE: Woof, woof, woof, woof! ⎦ (As he synchronizes with the teacher, some children laugh.)

Mrs. Barker found ways to keep Pierre positively engaged by making his assertive and idiosyncratic way of expressing his knowledge relevant to the activity. In the course of doing that, she was able to combine his pantomime and sound effects with her own language and use of concrete materials to showcase meanings for the entire class. She recognized the expressive capabilities that he brought to her classroom, even if they were not fully developed yet, and even if his own purposes did not coincide with her own agenda for his learning. Their initial partnership facilitated a closer alignment between his behavior and her agenda for Pierre's learning when he began to replace the sound effects with language that closely resembled the teacher's.

Showcasing Meanings as Teacher's Partner

This evolution in Pierre's participation in the partnership was evident on Day 78, as he and Mrs. Barker momentarily operated as a team.

> Mrs. Barker is having the children help her identify and label the opposites in Hoban's picture book *Exactly the Opposite* (1990). When Mrs. Barker shows the "back and front" picture, saying "This is the front," Pierre anticipates the opposite and says, "Back." As Mrs. Barker repeats the sequence "front and back," Pierre gradually adopts her rhythm of delivery. Then he joins her in a live display of front and back: Mrs. Barker stands up, gesturing to her front and then turning her back. With the next repetition, Pierre is up and beside her, and in perfect synchrony they present first their fronts and then their backs to the whole class.

T: ... This is the front.
PIERRE: Back.
T: Front, and this is the – – –
PIERRE: Ba::ck. ⎤
PETER: Back, back, back. ⎦
T: Front and back. ⎤
PIERRE: back. ⎦ Front.
T: Front and – – – (T has gotten up and is turning herself).
CHILDREN: Back. (Pierre gets up and joins the T.)
T/PIERRE: Front – – and – – back. (In synchrony and with a flourish,
    they present their fronts and then turn their backs. The
    children chuckle.)
T: Thank you, Pierre. (He sits down.)

During the above activities, Mrs. Barker gave Pierre's tendency to dramatize through pantomime and sound effects a legitimate role in highlighting meanings. Instead of squelching his high-profile dramatic tendencies, she treated them as valuable expressive resources. Their dramatic partnership modeled for Pierre the possibility of another kind of "partnership"—that between dramatic action and language in expressing meanings. At first, it was the teacher who supplied the words that were synchronized to Pierre's dramatic action. However, by the time of the "front/back" experience, Pierre himself was combining the action with the words. This acted as a scaffold for Pierre to extend his expressive repertoire in these Group Time activities, so that he began to incorporate the teacher's vocabulary in his increasingly verbal responses.

Refining His Verbal Responses

On Day 91, Mrs. Barker used a different book, Kightley's *Opposites* (1986), as a focus for the concepts. By this time, Pierre's incorporation of the teacher's vocabulary was consistently evident in his pattern of ending the discussion of specific pairs of opposites with a statement of the pair. Here are two of many examples:

T: In – –
JANINE: and out.
T: Yes. He's going in and coming out. ⎤
PIERRE: In and out. In and out.   ⎦

T: This sheep is – –
CHILDREN: Big. (Then T points to the small one.) Little.

T: Or small. Yes. Little is what it says.
PIERRE: Big 'n small. Big 'n small.

As Pierre's participation became more exclusively verbal, Mrs. Barker began to up the ante, letting Pierre know that she expected him to be more precise in his use of descriptive language. For example, on Day 108, she approached the concept of opposites through activities based on Frank Asch's *Short Train, Long Train* (1992). When Pierre repeatedly used the word *big* instead of *long* as the opposite of *short*, Mrs. Barker made a point of steering him to adopt her exact vocabulary.

T: Now we have a long train. Now we need something short. Let's look at the pictures (which "unfold" from short to long). Short train. Long train. Short nose – – –
PIERRE: Big nose.
T: Lo:ng.
DANIEL: I like a long nose.
T: Short dog – –
PIERRE: Big dog.
CHILD: Lo:::ng.
T: (locking eyes with Pierre) *Long* dog.
PIERRE: Long dog.

Pierre's characteristic language-and-action way of turning toward the teacher's read-alouds and task demonstrations affected the tone of those activities, injecting an air of excitement that might easily deteriorate into giddiness. Lindfors (1999) poses a question in terms of inquiry's purpose and expression that has relevance here in terms of Pierre's characteristic ways of responding in Group Time activities: "[W]ho has the right to set the tone, the way of turning toward the topic and toward each other? These are power questions."

PARTNERING WITH THE TEACHER TO
DESIGN PATHS FOR LEARNING

In Mrs. Barker's Group Time activities, she allowed assertive children such as Pierre and Inga leeway to set the tone to some extent. Instead of squelching Pierre's way of "turning toward the topic" of her read-alouds, Mrs. Barker began to incorporate some of the tone and style of his responses into her own dramatic delivery during these activities. Thereby, she channeled his highly stimulating, very visible, and frequently funny (at least to his peers) physical and vocal responses into the service of making her own presentations more understandable to the whole group. Perhaps the teacher's willingness to do so stems from the fact that Pierre's style as a performer was compatible with her own dramatic delivery, although all teachers who are dramatic do not necessarily readily take on partners from amongst their students.

But Mrs. Barker seemed to be very good at making positive use of very high profile behaviors that were not strictly "model student" behaviors. Mrs. Barker was able to recognize the relevance of Pierre's performative style and Inga's persistent questioning and imaginative scenarios to the accomplishment of some of her language-learning and content goals.

Inga's spontaneous creation of the visually compelling "growing flowers" scenario took place at a transition time, when the teacher had asked children to sit in their chairs and put their heads down; yet it met with no reprimands. Although the teacher established a clear set of daily routines and norms for behavior in the classroom, there was nevertheless space for spontaneous displays involving meanings to be shared by all. Boundaries were clear and strong, but also flexible, and children could both depend on the structural regularities in the classroom and on being allowed space to express themselves.

A lot has been written about how children catch on to norms for language use and attentive behaviors during teacher-directed Group Time activities, and about how teachers help them to do this (Cazden, 1988; Saville-Troike, 1985; Wong Fillmore, 1982, 1985). In the episodes featured in this chapter, Pierre and Inga had a hand in shaping the norms for interactions in their classroom, as they sought to legitimize their own preferred ways of responding, and the teacher seemed quite open to their efforts. Thus norms for language use and attentive behaviors evolved in collaboration between Mrs. Barker and the children.

Dyson (1999), in her discussion of transfer, emphasizes how essential it is for teachers not to overlook the resources children bring to the learning process, even if they are not those resources that the teacher would traditionally have in mind from her or his own frame of reference. Mrs. Barker did not look at the children only in terms of how far along *her* designated path they had come. She had the expectation that the children as individuals would to some extent design *their own* path. This was not to her an aberration, a special accommodation that she might make for one or two children who didn't fit her idea of a model student. She seemed to see it as a natural part of their being who they were.

5

Nobody Owns the Words: Capitalizing on Teacher Talk

On the morning of Day 1, Mrs. Barker is showing children where to sit in her classroom.

> T: Where's Francia? This is Francia's chair. (Francia sits.) Where is Tracy? Tracy, come here. This is Tracy's chair. (Tracy sits.) Where is Sue? This is Sue's chair. (Sue sits.)

As Mrs. Barker introduced children to their permanent place at a table, there was no trace of the unnaturally stilted cadence, exaggerated enunciation, or slightly too loud volume that people sometimes adopt when addressing those who may not understand their language. She was using a traditional ESL strategy of consistently associating familiar language patterns with particular routines or lesson segments (Wong Fillmore, 1985) so that ELLs would be supported in connecting classroom events and language.

On ensuing days, when Mrs. Barker called the children to morning Group Time, she would consistently use the phrase, "Come sit on the floor, children." Her consistency enabled children to rely on her words to figure out what was happening and what to do about it. But this consistency also served another function. Because the patterned phrases occurred predictably in specific situations—somewhat like the script associated with a particular scene in a drama—they entered the children's expressive repertoire as *stock phrases* that they could adapt and use in similar situations, either real or re-created in their play. These stock phrases, together with the associated activity formats and classroom routines, are what I refer to as *scripts*.

ENABLING CHILDREN TO RELY ON THE WORDS

Mrs. Barker served as a key resource for language learning in her classroom as the main "bearer" of words, because of the fact that she was the only native English speaker. The regularities of her scripts made her English more accessible to the children, both in terms of their understanding and in terms of their speaking English themselves. This chapter describes the characteristic ways that individual children relied on and used her scripts to support their own learning and participation in classroom events, to make sense of their school experiences, and to support peer interaction in English. Some of the ways that the children used these regularities as a resource were anticipated by the teacher, and some were less directly linked to specific teacher intentions.

Language Patterns as an Aid to Decoding

Yakov's interactions with Mrs. Barker about the routine of getting dressed to go home revealed that he was paying particular attention to the language patterns that Mrs. Barker consistently used in that situation. This language became recognizable to him as a script, a set of stock phrases whose meaning he came to understand from the context. Mrs. Barker always announced, "Boys, get dressed," followed after a short interval by "Girls, get dressed," or vice versa. At the end of Day 44, Yakov began to use a confirmation check for his understanding of that script. He reacted to Mrs. Barker's announcement, "Boys, get dressed," by approaching first me and then the teacher with the question: "I /gyet/ dressed?" He repeated this procedure on several different days, and Mrs. Barker replied, "You are a boy. Yes," or, as on Day 52, "You are a boy. You have to get dressed." By Day 57, when Mrs. Barker announced, "Boys, get dressed," Yakov immediately looked up at her and, gesturing to himself, asserted firmly, "I boy!" As he turned away to get his jacket, he somehow left me with the impression that he had just put in the last piece of a puzzle.

Yakov showed he understood how this script could be adapted to another classroom situation on Day 78. When Mrs. Barker called the girls to come and get paper for their art project, Alec, a new boy in the class, started to get up with the girls. Yakov turned to him and said, "You're not a girl!"

Lesson Formats as Cues for Participation

In one particularly striking instance, Robert capitalized on the teacher's consistency of format to support his participation in the Letter of the Week activity at morning Group Time. Whenever Mrs. Barker introduced the

Letter of the Week Alphabet Chart, she would signal this activity by pulling forward the easel with the chart and positioning it in such a way that
the children all had to turn slightly to face it. Then she would say, "Okay,
let's take a look at the alphabet." She would always begin with A, point to
"big A" and "small a," and have the children read as she pointed to each *A*
word and to the picture a child had drawn to go with it. When Mrs. Barker
reached the blank page reserved for the new Letter of the Week, she would
always, when possible, select a child whose name began with that letter
to write it at the top of the page.

Robert, who often stayed at his seat during alphabet activities, revealed
both his literacy knowledge and his familiarity with the format when he
chose his moment to join the children during the first day of R week. He
reminded me of an actor waiting for his cue to come onto the set.

> During the Alphabet Chart activity on Day 91, the first day of
> R week, Robert starts out sitting at his table, where he cannot see
> the chart. As Inga suggests her last name "Potasnik" for letter P,
> Robert stands up and stretches. When Mrs. Barker asks what comes
> after Q, he is making his way over to the circle. He reaches the
> circle precisely when Mrs. Barker says, "Big R, small r, Robert,
> come draw big R."

Mrs. Barker's predictable patterns helped Yakov and Robert to gauge
appropriate responses to teacher talk and to teacher-directed activities.
Yakov used the language patterns associated with particular events very
methodically to decode the teacher's procedural language, and Robert used
the activity formats to support his participation in Group Time activities.
Each capitalized on the teacher-provided regularities in his own way.

HELPING CHILDREN OWN THE WORDS

For Mrs. Barker to carry out to the fullest the role of "bearer of words,"
she had to find ways for children to take ownership of those words. Therefore, she did not regard her teacher talk as belonging to her exclusively.
She wanted the children to appropriate her vocabulary into activities beyond the boundaries of teacher-directed group activities and teacher-child
interactions. So, for example, she purposely fostered links between her
language during Group Time experiences and the children's language in
subsequent peer-mediated interaction. Mrs. Barker would introduce key
vocabulary in task demonstrations with concrete objects just before children made a transition from Group Time to Table Activities. For instance,

on Day 81, she showcased the vocabulary *first, second,* and *third* as she demonstrated how to make the three pigs' houses and pig stick-puppets for acting out *The Three Little Pigs* (1989). This vocabulary then played a part in children's informal discussions at their tables as they engaged in their tasks.

> T: You're gonna get three houses.
> . . .
> T: Now the first house to be built is the house made of straw. (puts it up on a board) Was this a strong house?
> GROUP: No.
> . . .
> T: The next house that was built is the house made of sticks, out of wood. Could he blow that one down?
> GROUP: Ye::s
> T: Yes. The second house was blown down. (puts second on board, and points to each) The first, second . . . and this is the third house. (puts it up on the board)
> CHILD: And stronger.
> T: (points to the houses) First, second, third. This is the strongest house. Remember you've gotta color them. Then you've gotta get the pigs to match the house. Where's the first little pig?

Soon after, Tracy, Jerry, and another child at their table are sorting out the houses at their table.

> CHILD: Where's the first house? Second house or first house?
> JERRY: (points) This uh this and this house.
> TRACY: Who's first house?
> JERRY: Uh this!
> TRACY: This one?
> JERRY: This first house.
> TRACY: This the first house?
> JERRY: Yes.
> TRACY: Where are number two house?
> JERRY: (points) This.
> . . .
> TRACY: (Finishes pasting the second house onto the paper, then picks up her last house.) Right! This is *three* house!

The vocabulary again came into play on Day 108, when Jerry discussed with Peter how to do two math workbook pages, This time, Jerry incorporated both *first* and *second* into his talk, as he said: "Peter, first draw a small one, second draw a big one, right?"

CHILDREN USING REGULARITIES FOR THEIR OWN PURPOSES

There were other reverberations of the teacher's regularities of routine and teacher talk which seemed less deliberately set in motion by the teacher, but which nonetheless had a powerful impact on children's engagement with each other and on children's mastery of curriculum.

Using Scripts for Routines as a Common Focus

Children began to use the predictable formats and patterned language from teacher talk during routines as scripts to support sustained interaction in English. They used these scripts with a shared sense of "getting through" to each other. For example, Penny ("Bing-ling") Chou and her tablemates played an Attendance Game that was very popular at individual tables and that also helped children identify their classmates early in the year:

> PENNY: Where's Ogusan, here? (points to his empty chair and
>   laughs) Ogusan go bathroom.
> PENNY: Robert? Robert? Robert?
> OLEG: He's absent
> PENNY: Pierre, Pierre, Pierre?
> OLEG: (points silently at Pierre)
> PENNY: Nesha?
> OLEG: Which Nesha?
> PENNY: Nesha is there. (points to Nesha at other table)

Savoring the Power of Teacher Talk

Sometimes these games came across as parodies of the classroom power structure. In the following variation on the Attendance Game, Penny and her tablemates seemed to be poking fun at the system of authority whereby the teacher, from the children's perspective, lorded it over them as they vied for the coveted opportunity to take a paper to the office after attendance.

> With a big grin on her face, Penny imitates the teacher's taking
> attendance, turning a page as she says each name.

PENNY: Good morning, Oleg, good morning, Galina.
OLEG: Galina absent.
PENNY: Good morning, Ogusan. (As she closes the book, the children all raise their hands in anticipation.)
PENNY: Oleg and Gennady, take this to the office.
PENNY: Raise your hand who comes / / office. (Oleg and Daniel raise their hands.)
PENNY: Oleg and Daniel, take it to the office. (They all giggle.)

In this variation on the Attendance Game, the children seemed to be appropriating not just the teacher's words, but the particular genre of teacher talk that Mrs. Barker's use of the words represented. The children perceived her procedural language—telling them what to do and selecting children to run errands—as a speech genre of power, and the children may well have heard an "echo" of her "individual expression" (Bakhtin, 1986) in their own use of that talk. Thus they appropriated not only her teacher talk, but the sense of power to "bestow favors" that those words had expressed when addressed to them. By reenacting the use of that genre in their Attendance Game, the children were able to savor the power and poke fun at it simultaneously.

In the following episode from later in the year, Tracy and Inga also appropriated not only the words but the power associated with teacher talk to induct Kaity and Julia into dramatic play in English. Kaity and Julia otherwise would habitually use only Chinese in dramatic play. The echo of the teacher's expressions made the words the children appropriated representative somewhat of Mrs. Barker's powerful status.

In this scenario in early December, Tracy assumed the role of Mrs. Barker, and Inga assumed the role of Mrs. Weinstein, Mrs. Barker's colleague next door. They divided the house corner into two parallel classrooms and each had their own class with one student. They positioned themselves so that they could see each other, and they incorporated some of the participation structures that Mrs. Barker had established at Group Time in their own classroom. When Inga read to her student Kaity, Tracy read to Julia. When Inga told her student to get on line, Tracy did the same. Only the dialogue between Tracy and Julia was fully transcribed.

Tracy holds up an empty record jacket, which she uses as a book. She asks Julia a series of "what" questions and gets her to label objects. Then she takes a large folded paper with illustrations and writing and teaches Julia from it.

TRACY: (points to letter V) Wee. Say "Wee."
JULIA: Wee.
TRACY: (points at U and then V) U, Veh, V, say "V."
JULIA: 'V.'
TRACY: You. Say "you."
JULIA: You.
TRACY: Can.
JULIA: Can.
TRACY: Play.
TULIA: Play.
. . .
TRACY: (starts to fold up the paper from which she has been teach-
       ing) This very very / /. Julia very very smart girl. (Tracy shows
       her the pictures.) You like it? (smiles) Finished.
TRACY: Okay. Look at me. We go to our bahthroom.

Particularly striking in this episode was Tracy's appropriation of Mrs. Barker's teacher talk and of participation structures familiar from Group Time to define and support Julia's English-speaking role. Tracy asked Julia to label things ("What's that?"), told her to repeat what the teacher says ("Say _____"), made evaluative comments at the end of the activity, reminded her to look at the teacher, and—just like Mrs. Barker—signaled the transition to Bathroom Time with the linguistic marker, "Okay." Tracy also imitated the teacher's British pronunciation of *bathroom*, and indulged in a language play on the sound of the letter *U* and the word *you*.

This type of creative appropriation was not part of Mrs. Barker's official agenda, but nonetheless was indirectly facilitated by her rendering the language and participation structures accessible to the children. The children, during their informal interaction in Mrs. Barker's classroom, had the freedom to take on roles and ways of talking characteristic of their teacher's normative classroom behavior. Cazden (1988) has characterized peer interaction as the social context with the optimum room for reversal of interactional roles: Children can give directions to peers instead of following them, as with the teacher; they can ask questions instead of just answering.

Using Teacher Talk as Authoritative Text

Children drew on another aspect of the regularities presented by the teacher to support their own fluency in monologues. These monologues usually consisted of oral emergent reading or retelling of an often-heard story, or reiteration of the teacher's script for enacting math problems, such as the "Which is more?" script described in Chapter 3. In this regard, Johnson (1994) refers to teacher talk as one kind of *authoritative text* that children use to support their language learning. As resources from the *textual sphere* category, she includes stories, teacher's lessons, and written texts. Johnson differentiates these resources from those in the *contextual sphere*, which draw more on the social knowledge that informs the informal ongoing peer interaction in the school. The "baby sleeping" joke between Inga, Tracy, and Jerry is one example of drawing primarily on the contextual sphere.

Tracy drew support from the textual sphere when she took on the role of teacher on Day 92 to conduct a read-aloud for an imaginary audience of peers. That day, Play Time was limited to books and puzzles. Tracy propped her big book up on the blackboard and began to "read" the story of *Goldilocks and the Three Bears* (1989):

> "D'you dri/ drink little bit?" " Sure I will drink little," Goldilocks say. (points to bowls in turn during this) "Oh dat is too hot. Dat is too cold. Dis is just right," Goldilocks say. Here she is. "So hard this chair," Goldilocks say. "This chair is so long. This chair is just right." Goldilocks say, "This bed is too /stoft/ [soft]." Goldilocks say, "This bed is too long, too soft." Goldilocks say, "This bed just right." Then he say, "This is first bed. I can't do //" he say, and he do bro' the Goldilocks chair, and he say he scarey. He say, "Who's do bro' my bed?" And Gra/ Goldilocks running comes out. Goldilocks, and de [the] end.
>   Oh, are you Goldilocks is good? No, she's not good.

Tracy's monologue gave her an opportunity to produce a very sustained flow of English, supported by text scripts that were very familiar both from Mrs. Barker's readings and from the acting out of the story in class. Her reading of *Goldilocks and the Three Bears* (1989) was quite accurate in terms of the page-by-page sequence of the story. She hadn't quite mastered the series of opposites needed for the telling, but she improvised. What was striking was that Tracy ended with a little coda, consisting of a question and answer sequence appropriated from the end of Mrs. Barker's own reading of the story to the class.

Inga drew support from the textual sphere on Day 70, when she tried out the role of Mrs. Barker teaching the math lesson on "which is more" referred to previously in Chapter 3. As she cleaned up the math manipulatives the teacher had used, Inga launched into a monologue incorporating some of the teacher's script. Here is an excerpt from the teacher's actual lesson, followed by Inga's adaptation.

T: (counting) One, two red shapes. Three red shapes. (T lines up
    three red shapes.) One, two, three, let's see one, two, three,
    four, five, blocks. (lines those up) Which one is more?
CHILD: Five.
CHILDREN: Fi::ve
T: Five is more than three. How many more?

INGA'S ADAPTATION

Inga: (sets up six blocks and three bunny counters, i.e., little plastic
    bunnies used for counting activities) Okay. What's more?
    (places each bunny counter on top of one of the blocks, and
    points to the blocks) That's more d'you understand? It's gonna
    be more. How much is dat? Three. 'Kay. One, two. Okay.
    Shapes. The shapes. I'm gonna do dis. (takes out five pentagon
    shapes and three of another kind) What's more, children?
    What's more? Five is more.

Challenging Peers with Teacher Talk

Not all adaptations of teacher talk for peer interaction involved taking
on the role of teacher. Sometimes during play, Jerry would appropriate
scripts from Mrs. Barker's lessons to support his role as a challenging peer.
In his literacy-related talk, he took a competitive stance toward peers,
urging them to try to match his knowledge or to display their own. At a
time in the school year when the teacher was beginning to highlight spelling of words during the Class News, Jerry brought spelling into his talk
with peers. In doing so, he seemed to incorporate the teacher's script
"How do you spell . . . ?" in relation to children's names, and the letter
quiz question "What's this?" in relation to identifying letters. In the following examples, it is as if the theme "Whose is bigger?" which was a
focus of arguments in some of Jerry's block play, reappeared as "Who
knows more?"

On Day 90, Jerry reacts to Inga's expression of surprise that Ilya
knew "her name Russian" by proclaiming: "I know he/ he [Ilya]
don' know my name how to spell!" Jerry follows up this statement
by pointing to each letter of his own name label and quizzing Ilya:
"What/s that? How 'bout dis one? What's dat? What's dat?"

Jerry twice issues a similar spelling challenge to Inga on Day 102,
when he sees her trying to write other children's names into her

pretend "attendance book" by copying their name labels. Each time, he uses a more standard word order than he did on Day 90. Covering his name label, he challenges: "You don't know how to spell my name. Spell my name. You don't know how to spell my name!"

Trying on a Literate Role with Teacher Talk

In these types of interactions, Jerry recontextualized the teacher talk in a frame of reference that suited his own social purposes. His use of English in these examples was supported not only by the teacher's script, but by his confidence in his own literacy knowledge. When he and Tracy entered kindergarten, they both revealed an easy familiarity with written symbols and with writing that Inga did not possess. Inga sometimes used teacher talk in her dramatic play to develop a framework in which knowing how to write would become personally relevant to her. She began to create challenges for herself as she incorporated increasingly specific and demanding literacy tasks into her assumed role as teacher. On Day 63, she created a monologue about attendance in which she pretended to write the names of absentees. She played both the role of teacher and the role of the children, disguising her voice for the role of children (when she speaks as a child, Inga's name will appear as "Inga").

INGA: Good morning. Good morning, Ogusan.
"INGA": Good morning, Mrs. Barker.
INGA: Good morning, Inga.
"INGA": Good morning, Mrs. Barker.
INGA: Good morning, Tracy. Absent one. [Tracy really is absent.]
    Good morning, Jason. Absent two. Two.
    Good morning, Yakov. Absent three.
    Good morning, Al-*the*-a (accents it like Mrs. Barker).
"INGA": Good morning, Mrs. Ba:::rker.
. . .
INGA: Today somebody absent. So I'm gonna // see something.
    (looks in her notebook) Ah. Here is who absent. (writes in her book) One ah um Yakov. (closes her "attendance" book)

When Inga played taking attendance again on Day 102, while sitting at her table during Rest Time–Homework Check, she tried to write down accurately the names of her absentees. She could only do this if her absentees all had name labels that she could see and copy. Since most of the absentees were actually sitting nearby at the table, Inga met with some resistance, particularly from Francia.

INGA: Okay. Good morning, Francia.

FRANCIA: Good morning.

INGA: Absent.

FRANCIA: No, I *here*.

INGA: I not gonna do everyone not absent. I not gonna *do* dat. *Ilya* absent. 'I'-'I'- (starts to copy his name down on the absent list)

FRANCIA: (to Ilya) Say good morning, Ilya! Good morning, Ilya! (She beckons him with her hand.)

ILYA: Good morning.

FRANCIA: (to Inga) She's [He's] not absent. He's *here*. (Inga copies Ilya's name from his table name label.)

INGA: Good morning, Tracy. Absent. [Tracy really was absent.] How you spell Tracy?

JERRY: T (Jerry covers Tracy's name label.)

INGA: (to Jerry) Stop closing the name. Sto::p. You don't have Play Time! I don't do this. You don't have Play Time! I tell the teacher!

JERRY: (uncovers label) Sorry.

FRANCIA: (to Inga) He say sorry.

INGA: (erasing, tells Jerry) It's all your fault.

JERRY: (watching Inga write Tracy's name) C here.

INGA: I *draw* C. (Inga is copying Tracy's name upside down and backwards, the way it looks to her while looking at Tracy's label from the other side of the table.)

. . .

JERRY: One more. You don't know how to spell my name. Spell my name. (covers his label) You don't know how to spell my name.

INGA: I don't need dat. Only girls' names and Ilya's name.

In her particular ways of appropriating the teacher's authoritative texts, Inga brought herself ever closer to the teacher's definition of literacy tasks, but deliberately structured the scenarios so as not to become overwhelmed by the tasks. In the above episode, only Jerry seemed aware that Inga's behavior was a literacy strategy, and he tried to foil her by covering up name labels. Toward the end of the episode, Jerry's purpose for appropriating the teacher's scripts (to challenge peers) clashed with Inga's purpose (to master a literacy task).

Litowitz (1993), in her discussion of *scaffolding*, suggests that "mastering activities and establishing a sense of oneself are not two distinct lines of development, but are, rather, entwined in complex ways—that one cannot 'study' one without the other" (p. 184). In this regard, Inga seems to be trying on the persona of teacher as a powerful figure who uses literacy as an important part of her role. This serves as motivation for Inga's own efforts to meet the challenges of learning to write. Litowitz continues, "Briefly, what motivates the child to master tasks is not the mastery itself but the desire to be the adult or to be the one the adult wants him to be" (p. 187). This kind of statement is consonant with Inga's taking on the teacher's role to support her literacy development and with Tracy's taking on the teacher's role to support her English fluency. But it does not shed any light on Jerry's appropriation of the teacher's scripts without taking on her role. His motivation seems directly rooted in his peer relationships.

6

Peer Support

INGA: (pointing repeatedly at Jerry's writing) I don' like *that*. I don' like *that*. I don' like *that*.

JERRY: (grinning, points back at hers) I don' like *this*. I don' like *this*. I don' like *this*.

INGA: I like *mine*. I don' like *yours*.

JERRY: So I don' like/ I like *mine*, not/not *you*! (Inga laughs.) (Day 42)

In this informal scene, mock evaluation at the table during writing practice served as an impetus for the children's repartee in English, and Jerry was trying hard to match the phrasing and rhythm of Inga's more fluent and colloquial English. This episode was one of many instances I documented of peer interaction that seemed to support getting into English. In classroom contexts where children could interact freely without direct mediation by the teacher, they helped each other begin to use English among a broadening network of peers, for an expanding variety of purposes, and—at least to some extent—with more precision.

Writing practice was an activity during which most of the teacher's comments were evaluative, although mostly positive and encouraging in nature. For the children, playfully trading critical remarks was a use of English which would not likely occur in interaction with a teacher. However, as was pointed out in Chapter 1, children have an opportunity in a playful context to expand their linguistic capital beyond language forms they would use with a teacher or other adult.

The preceding chapter described ways in which children appropriated teacher talk and predictable activity formats for their own purposes in monologues and in peer interactions. This chapter examines more extensively peer interactions in contexts where communication was unmediated by the teacher. The examples presented document the impressive range of strategies among peers that supported increased use of English with at least some trend toward more precise expression, more complex, elaborated sentences, and more standard form.

FOSTERING COMMUNICATION ACROSS LANGUAGE BACKGROUNDS

Many early uses of English were embedded in children's sociability—their eagerness to communicate and their efforts to cultivate friendships. This was particularly evident in interactions involving Jerry, Inga, and Tracy, who all sat at one end of the same table. Jerry sat directly across from Tracy, and Inga sat next to Jerry. They used a number of different strategies that fostered peer communication across language backgrounds.

At the beginning of the school year, Jerry and Tracy, the only Cantonese speakers at their table (Eve spoke Fu Chow Chinese), sat across from each other and represented potentially one of those isolated islands of home language use that some fear may delay children's getting into English. They usually conversed in Cantonese at Snack Time, during art and writing tasks, and during play with manipulatives at the table. However, Inga, who was one of several Russian speakers at the table, was not easily deterred from attempting to join in on their Cantonese conversations, using English as a lingua franca.

In the third week of school, she listened and watched closely as Tracy and Jerry had a discussion in Cantonese about what Eve had written on her picture. She heard the word Eve and saw Tracy touch the name on Eve's picture, and also Eve's table name label. When Tracy and Jerry paused, Inga offered this contribution: "She no did this (touching Eve's last name on her table name label); she did this (touching Eve's first name), not this (touching the last name)."

Inga used another tactic that week to break into their Cantonese conversation when the topic of their talk was less transparent. She leaned across the table toward Tracy and asked, "What's my name? What's my name? I can do my name."

Inga's assertiveness with Tracy and Jerry worked against their functioning as an isolated Cantonese-speaking duo at their table. Her persistence extended to frequent haggling with them over snacks. On one such occasion, Jerry's deft codeswitching between fluent Cantonese and less fluent English also contributed to keeping all three children in a joint conversational loop.

JERRY: (to Inga) You have dis? (points to his cheese doodles) Your house? Your house. My mother buy this.

INGA: I have. Because I don't taste it any more, Mommy don't buy me dis anymore.

JERRY: (to Inga) My Mommy bought dis. (turning to Tracy) MY SISTER BOUGHT IT FOR ME. WHY YOUR SISTER DON'T BUY FOR YOU?

. . .

INGA: (to Jerry) Can I have one?

JERRY: No more.

INGA: You're not gonna have my cookies.

JERRY: (loud) Okay. One more time. No mo'.

INGA: Okay

JERRY: (to Tracy, with his mouth full.) No more. Almost finished. I'M NOT GIVING OUT ANY MORE [cheese doodles].

Once during the episode, Jerry translated into English for Inga what Tracy had just said, and used that to launch a new line of argument with Inga:

TRACY: (to Jerry) MOMMY TELLS ME TO PLAY BY MYSELF. I DON'T KNOW WHY.

JERRY: (to Inga) Her Mommy tell him [Tracy] – – – tell him not be my friend. Mommy tell him. Not be *his* friend, okay? [Don't be her friend.]

ESTABLISHING ENGLISH AS A LINGUA FRANCA IN PLAY

The reader may recall that in Chapter 5 Tracy and Inga used the authority role of teacher to establish English as the lingua franca for dramatic play with Julia and Kaity, who habitually limited themselves to interactions in Cantonese. In such efforts, Tracy did not restrict herself to the teaching role, but cloaked herself in other authoritative roles. In the following episode in early December, she took on the powerful role of doctor. Throughout the play, she kept up a running commentary in English about checking the babies, giving them medicine, and scheduling another appointment. While Kaity and Julia used some Cantonese during the play, Tracy tried to reserve Cantonese for moments when she wanted to make sure Kaity and Julia understood what was supposed to happen:

TRACY: (to Julia) I'm doctor, okay? I'M A DOCTOR.

. . .

TRACY: (holding doll on lap and smiling) Baby. Look. Is a beautiful.

JULIA: Beautiful.

TRACY: Say "Hi!"
JULIA: Hi!

Rephrasing was another strategy Tracy used to get her meaning across to them in English, as she experimented with different ways of framing her suggestion: "Okay. We go. We may go home. Oh. Do we go home now. Le's go home."

COLLABORATING IN IMAGINATIVE MINISCENARIOS

By early October it was evident that Inga, Tracy, and Jerry were discovering the sheer pleasure of sharing humorous perceptions in English, as all three collaborated in developing the "baby sleeping" joking narrative based on their common understanding of school routines. This pleasure in sharing perceptions eventually led to collaborative miniscenarios in which they shared symbolic imagery created through English. During the *Three Little Pigs* art project in late January, Inga set a collaboration in motion, this time expressing an image in words, not pantomime. The children were each coloring a straw, a wood, and a brick house for their own puppet show scenery. As Inga colored her brick house black, she came up with the idea of a light in the house. Jerry and Tracy both responded separately to Inga's idea, although Tracy's response was not fully available in the transcription because parts were inaudible. In Jerry's comment, he extended Inga's idea.

INGA: It's a light in the house. (jumps up and down) It's a light
– – – in the house.
. . .
JERRY: (talking about his picture to Res) He [the pig] don't open the
light. He sleeping.
RES: Uhuh.
INGA: [about the house Tracy is coloring black] Your too done
beautiful.
TRACY: My house, the light //.

At Snack Time on February 4th, it was Jerry who provided the theme for a scenario in which the three children again collaborated. Inga had been comparing the size of Tracy's, Jerry's, and her own drink boxes. Jerry's was largest, Inga's was slightly smaller, and Tracy's was the smallest. Jerry then compared the boxes to a family and they all acted out a miniscenario:

JERRY: (to Inga and Tracy) I mommy father baby. (pointing to the drink boxes)

TRACY: (to Inga) // I'm baby crying, whaaah. What // say [to] daughter?

INGA: (to Tracy) Daughter, why ya crying?

TRACY: (to Jerry) Jerry, the fader [father] come back.

INGA: (to Jerry) Father, come. Daughter want you. Wake up. (His juice box is lying down on its side on the table.)

JERRY: (to Inga and Tracy) I not up. *Up*. Help me out. Come on!

GIVING AND RECEIVING SUPPORT: REVERSAL OF ROLES

In the growing friendship between the children, there were many occasions when one child was on the giving end and one on the receiving end of support, bearing out the notion of scaffolding by a more capable peer. But the role of giver and receiver changed with different conversational partners and in different situations.

It was very evident early in the year that Inga's English was more colloquial than Tracy's. For example, when Inga sought reassurance while assembling pieces of a puppet, she asked me, "Are these cute?" in contrast to Tracy's very understandable but less colloquial, "Like these the *good*?" Tracy, like Jerry, often seemed to use Inga's greater fluency as a resource, and imitated her speech over a whole range of classroom contexts, from Group Time to Table Activities, during transitions, on line, and at play. Tracy's imitation was not as a private echoing, but as a coparticipation in Inga's interactions with the teacher (Teacher, we have to dress?), peers (No talking during a fire drill!), and in repartee with each other (I have *this*!).

Although Tracy's English was less colloquial than Inga's, Tracy was able to provide Inga with corrective feedback about color labels. Early in November (Day 55), children at their table were discussing what color body they were going to pick for their dog puppets. The construction paper bodies were piled in the middle of the table. Inga announced, "I'm gonna take this yellow," and picked up an orange body. She continued, "I'm gonna take yellow. If you wanna take yellow, you can take yellow." In the ensuing conversation, Tracy gave her corrective feedback:

TRACY: You wanna yellow? Okay. Go take yellow. Yellow one *I* take. Yellow. I need yellow please.

INGA: Yellow. (holds up an orange one)

TRACY: No. *Dat* one yellow. (points to a yellow one) You wanna yellow?

There were other incidents in which Inga was on the receiving end of support from peers. One of her strengths in negotiating shared meaning with peers was her ability to use pantomime skillfully to supplement her English vocabulary. This allowed her, for example, in conversations with Tracy, to give a glimpse of her home life, as in this brief description late in October: "My father do every day like this (she swung a doll way up in the air and down again several times) and me do like this—ha ha!"

However, Inga's penchant for using pantomime to supplement her English could not help her in situations where the pleasure was in the familiar rhythmic chanting of the text from a predictable book. One such situation on Day 22 was an occasion for a spontaneous collaborative read-aloud with Penny supplying the needed vocabulary. Both children wanted the one classroom copy of *Brown Bear, Brown Bear* (Martin, 1983) during an informal individual reading time; Inga grabbed the book, but just as suddenly made room for Penny to share her chair. After Penny sat down with a surprised smile, Inga kept a firm grip on the book, holding it aloft, pursing her lips, and posturing importantly as she started to "read" aloud. Every time she paused, at a loss for a word, Penny quietly and with perfect timing, provided the right word, and Inga smoothly incorporated the prompt into her reading.

INGA: I see neigh neigh looking at me. What da you see? I see a – –
PENNY: Gray mouse.
INGA: looking at me. – – –
PENNY: Gray mouse.
INGA: Gray mouse what do you see?
. . .
INGA: I see da cat looking at me.
PENNY: Purple cat.
INGA: Purple cat, purple cat what do you see? I see the – – –
PENNY: Pink elephant.
INGA: Pink elephant looking at me.

DRAWING ON MINIRESERVOIRS OF CIRCULATING VOCABULARY

The children's abiding interest in each other's business led to spontaneous language practice, during which a particular pool of vocabulary circulated among peers. Jerry and his tablemates, while minding each other's business, seemed unwittingly to create spontaneous mini–language practice sessions with a core topic-related vocabulary. Jerry often seemed to draw support for his English use from minireservoirs of vocabulary circulating among peers who shared a common focus of attention.

A shared focus on Day 90 was Jerry's missing candy, and the circulating vocabulary seemed a cross between a conjugation of the verb *to take* and a real-life variation on the chant: "Who stole the cookie from the cookie jar? *X* (insert child's name) stole the cookie from the cookie jar. Who me? Yes you. Not me. Then who?" (The children had not learned the chant in school.)

INGA: (to Jerry) Where's your candy?
JERRY: I put candy over he::re. Who take it?
INGA: I don't know. Maybe Tracy. Tracy you taking his candy?
TRACY: No.
INGA: Then who took it?
JERRY: Who take it me?
TRACY: I don' take it. I don't take. Inga, I just see it right?
INGA: Yeh, I just lookin' in everywhere. Every every-where. And
       it's not here. I looked in my desk.
TRACY: Maybe Annie take it.
INGA: Maybe uh Annie sister.
JANINE: Annie did not take it, Jerry.
JERRY: (to Inga) My candy not here. Annie not take it. He not
       take it.
INGA: Then who maybe take it? – – – – – – – – – – – Yeh I see she
       take it.
JERRY: Francia, you taking my candy I put in here?
JANINE: No. Annie said no. Her not take it.
JERRY: I said Francia.
JANINE: No. How 'bout Ilya? Ilya // Tracy, when it was his birthday.
TRACY: He take it?
CHILD: He took two candies.
TRACY: I forgot to tell my mommy fader [father].
JERRY: I tell my/ my Mommy – – take – a my candy.

PUSHING A PEER TO ELABORATE

The children's growing curiosity about each other and growing sense of how to get a rise out of one another also led to their pushing each other to elaborate and clarify their English. As the children got to know each other better, there was often a competitive edge to the ways in which they used that knowledge to get a rise out of one another. Sometimes this knowledge of what would provoke a peer led to "gushes" of longer sentences in English. For example, early in February, Tracy's assertion that she was "bigger 'n" Jerry evoked from him a stream of English to negate her claim:

> TRACY: Jerry, I'm bigger 'n you. Let's see.
> JERRY: Let's see. (They stand forehead to forehead to measure.)
> TRACY: I'm bigger 'n you.
> JERRY: (to Inga) No. She cheating. On his foot. (demonstrates standing on tiptoe.) I/ she do this. She do this. She do like this. Tomorrow ha/ I happy birth/ I happy birthday the seven. I'm six.
> TRACY: In January what?
> JERRY: No, in June. This is May June July. This is happy birthday. June happy birthday on me.

That same day, during a Chinese New Year celebration, Tracy's curiosity about Jerry's interaction with the teacher led her to push him to elaborate and clarify his English. When Mrs. Barker invited Jerry, Inga, and Tracy to come and take "Cantonese cakes" [donuts] they had all baked, Inga and Tracy each came back with a cake, but Jerry came back empty-handed and explained: "Miz Barker byebye. I don't wanta cake. I don't want a cake. She say 'Byebye.'" Tracy seemed quite taken aback that he actually refused the teacher's invitation outright, and wanted to know exactly what he said:

> TRACY: You not wanna eat?
> JERRY: I don't wanta eat. Miz Barker say, "Byebye."
> TRACY: You say, "I don' wanna eat you can put in the garbage?" You say what?
> JERRY: I not take it. I say, "I don' wanta take it." She say, "Okay, don't take it. Byebye." I go "eh." I go "uh oh."

After Tracy and Inga actually tasted the Cantonese cakes, they decided they didn't want to eat them either and experimented with sarcastic use of the word "delicious."

> TRACY: Delicious.
> INGA: Delicious.
> TRACY: Let's put it in the garbage.

Inga: (makes a disgusted face) Really delicious. (watches Tracy and
    laughs)
Tracy: (takes a bite and makes a disgusted face) Yucky! (spits it
    out) Inga, do you wanna eat? You say "Missa Barker, I don'
    wanna eat." Just tell her. Just tell her. (Tracy goes to throw
    hers in the garbage.)
Inga: I put it in the garbage with throwing it. (covers it with a
    napkin) Nothing in there. (goes to throw it in the garbage)

In daring Inga to be frank with the teacher, Tracy created embedded
dialogue, used a variety of sentence structures—statements, questions, and
imperatives—and accurately included a variety of pronouns.

These vignettes document Jerry, Inga, and Tracy's use of strategies
that tapped peer support for getting into English. Of the other case study
children, Pierre was most similar to Tracy, Inga, and Jerry in using peer
interaction to explore negotiation of shared meaning in English. Pierre
used superhero play to sustain interaction with his peers. He and his
sword-wielding playmates progressed over a period of months through
several stages of interaction in English from (1) trading onomatopoeic
traffic and animal sounds to (2) addressing each other in "macho" voices
as Ninja turtle characters to (3) discussing the attributes of their super-
heroes (Power/ Power Ranger man can' [can't?] fly. Right? . . . What
Power Ranger do?) to (4) more complex arguments in English about who
would be which "Power Ranger." Early in the year, Pierre mixed French
grammar and vocabulary into his talk, saying, for example, "'fait' l'again"
for "do it again." None of the children were observed to imitate these
constructions; however, Pierre heard others use the words *make* and *do*
very often during art activities, and gradually replaced '*fait*' with *do*.

CONSTRAINTS ON PEER SUPPORT

Although Yakov sat at the same table as Inga, Tracy, and Jerry, he did not
access peer support in the same way and to the same extent as they did.
When Yakov began to use some English after conversing only in Russian
for the first few weeks of school, he confined his efforts initially almost
exclusively to interaction with the teacher. For most of the year Yakov, in
his play, was defensive rather than collaborative, and used commands in
English for guarding his turf and possessions. During the second half of
the study, he used English often to tell Ilya, another Russian-speaking
tablemate, how to do academic tasks. For these "tutorials," he appropriated the teacher's directions for tasks as his script.

Robert actually exhibited a personal preference to rely on his peers rather than on the teacher as a resource for interaction, but at his table these peers all spoke his home language, and it was only very late in the year that he responded to overtures of peers from other home language groups who addressed him in English.

At his small table of only Cantonese speakers, Robert did not explore negotiating shared meaning in English during Table Activities. Materials such as *Three Little Pigs* paper houses, which spawned questions, comments, and symbolic imagery in English at Jerry, Inga, and Tracy's table, did not serve as an impetus for exploring communication in English at Robert's table. Nor did the need to share art materials, which Mrs. Barker built into Table Activities, foster use of English among Robert and his tablemates. Like Jerry, Inga, and Tracy, they played, argued, criticized, discussed tasks, negotiated over materials, and joked, but all in Cantonese.

Mrs. Barker felt, upon reflection, that while Robert's seatmates provided him with positive emotional, social, and academic support, the lack of additional seatmates from other language backgrounds may well have played a role in delaying his use of English with peers. The following year, she replaced the circular table with a rectangular one that could be clustered with other tables, providing more grouping flexibility.

ROBERT GETTING PULLED INTO PLAY IN ENGLISH

Robert's negotiation of shared meaning in English took place with non-Cantonese-speaking peers during Play Time late in the study. Robert rarely sought out non-Cantonese speakers as play partners. But Daniel, an Albanian speaker who habitually used English in school, sought Robert out and worked hard to establish a shared focus of attention with him on more than one occasion late in the study. In one such episode involving play with unifix blocks and number cards, Daniel's role was reminiscent of the scaffolding role a parent might take in trying to involve a very young child in verbal interaction. Without encroaching on Robert's purposive use of the materials, Daniel supplied a "language bath" (Urzua, 1989). He treated their play explicitly as an interactive game ("This's how we play"), applauded Robert's accomplishments ("Ya::::y!"), described the number cards they were finding ("Hey! Over here's four!"), explicitly bid for his attention ("Ay, look at dis!"), and asked questions about what Robert was doing ("You're up to six?"). Robert, proving responsive to these efforts, began to talk out loud in English about what he was doing, and began modeling some of his exclamations and questions after Daniel's.

This chapter has featured the many strategies children used to support each other's L2 learning. The vignettes featuring Inga, Tracy, and Jerry showed children breaking down the isolation of enclaves of home language speakers, using home languages to broaden the network of English speakers, providing opportunities for language practice, creating imaginative scenarios with words, and supporting more fluent, more elaborate, or more sophisticated uses of English. These three children and Pierre took full advantage of the opportunities Mrs. Barker gave them to participate in informal peer interaction—with freedom to explore ways of communicating in pursuit of social goals. Yakov's preference to use the adults as a predominating resource was a constraint on his using similar strategies, and Robert's seating arrangement made his choices for getting into English more limited.

CONTEXT-SPECIFIC STRATEGIES FOR PEER SUPPORT

All these children were L2 learners, and no one child could consistently serve as a "more proficient model" of English language use for another child. Thus Jerry, Inga, and Tracy, for example, did not fall into neat categories of "more proficient" or "less proficient" English speaker in their relationships with fellow L2-learning peers. However, the individual strengths that they each brought to particular conversations made positive contributions to each other's learning.

The children at different times and in different situations enacted roles of both the good language learner and the good language facilitator. Inga, Tracy, Pierre, and Jerry all used tactics associated with the good language learner (Gomez, 1987): placing themselves where they could hear English spoken, listening and watching as others conversed, asking questions and making comments, and attracting attention to themselves. Inga, Tracy, and Jerry, in particular, created many opportunities to practice their English with each other. Moreover, Inga, Tracy, Pierre, Jerry, and Daniel incorporated into their interactions a focus on substance over form, a shared focus on concrete objects such as snacks, drink boxes, and art materials as a pretext for talk, and all supplemented their language with pantomime, gesture, facial expression, sound effects, and demonstrations.

Inga, Tracy, and Daniel also used strategies identified with friendly, playful native-speaking facilitators (Gomez, 1987) by persistently engaging peers in conversation during a variety of activities, about a variety of things, and using a variety of linguistic structures. In addition, restatements, expansions, and corrective feedback were all parts of Tracy's and Daniel's repertoires.

A MODEL OF PEER COLLABORATION

These examples of peer support were characterized by a very distinctive feature, namely, the social energy that fueled the children's efforts. The example of repartee between Jerry and Inga that opened this chapter highlights this feature. The fact that Inga's participation provided a model of English phrasing and rhythmic expression for Jerry to try to emulate was an unintended beneficial by-product of their playful exchanges. Such unintended bonuses for L2 learning are reminiscent of opportunities for literacy learning described by Dyson (1987) among young native English speakers. She discusses the potential of peer interactions to "provide both social support and social energy—the capacity for action fueled by human desire for social communication and individual expression" (p. 397). Her two sets of case studies (1989, 1993) highlight the specific informal social contexts surrounding children's composing time, in which children supported each other's integration of writing into their repertoire of communicative and social tools. As in Mrs. Barker's classroom, the teachers in Dyson's studies legitimized the children's interest in one another; although the children's goals in spontaneous peer talk were not always driven by the teacher's agenda, often valuable literacy learning was embedded in their spontaneous verbal exchanges. In their interactions, their pushing the limits of each other's understanding paralleled to some extent my case study children's pushing the limits of each other's linguistic resources.

Among the case study children—particularly Jerry, Inga, and Tracy— curiosity about each other, growing knowledge of each other, and deepening friendships seemed often to provide the impetus for increased use of English in their interactions. The children's reaching out to one another also provided the "push to elaborate" that Swain (1985) projects as so necessary in getting children to improve their productive use of L2. Tracy's fascination with Jerry's outright refusal to accept Mrs. Barker's offer of a Cantonese cake was a striking example of a child's pushing a peer to elaborate, and—in the process—elaborating herself. In an atmosphere where children had a chance to talk and get to know "what made each other tick," talk engendered more talk.

Much of that talk gave the children opportunities to expand their linguistic capital by using forms of language that they would be unlikely to use in interactions with the teacher. These forms for nurturing, negotiating, persuading, arguing, and questioning were all exhibited by the children. Nurturing forms characterized Daniel's interactions with Robert, negotiation and arguing characterized Inga's haggling over snacks with Tracy and Jerry as well as Jerry's interactions with peers about "who's bigger," and persuading and questioning were at the heart of Tracy's persistence with peers over the Cantonese cakes. These vignettes seem to corroborate Ervin-Tripp's (1991) citing of evidence that "children can be highly motivated in arguments to push their language resources to elaboration" (p. 91).

In Ervin-Tripp's (1991) study of peer interaction among young L1 and L2 learners, she found that peers are sometimes more likely than adults to tailor their interaction sensitively to other children's interests and language level. For instance, she cited the kind of imitative, repetitive language play that children often enjoy, but of which an adult might soon tire. The imitative language play between Inga and her tablemates Jerry and Tracy fall into this category, as does the prolonged discussion of Jerry's missing candy among the children. The very limited store of English phrases that circulated in the missing candy episode helped to sustain talk in English, as children established and maintained a shared focus of attention.

The reciprocal model of peer scaffolding suggested by Dyson and Ervin-Tripp seems a good fit to the many peer collaborations documented in Mrs. Barker's classroom. Tracy and Inga both inducted other Cantonese-speaking children into dramatic play in English, when they would not undertake it on their own initiative. Children helped each other to "read" out loud, to bring the teacher's language into their play, and—with the aid of shared visible referents and imagination—to create imaginative scenarios with words, such as in the "drink box family" episode. In sum, children collaborated with peers of both like and different backgrounds to help each other do many things with language they could not originally do on their own. When children were given ample opportunities to create their own frames of reference for interaction with each other, many of their interactions were compatible with their teacher's goals for second-language learning.

7

Yakov: A Different Timetable and His Own Agenda

On Day 22, while Mrs. Barker is conducting a Group Time discussion of the calendar, Yakov suddenly looms in front of her chair holding in front of her face a small scrap of paper. "Garbage?" he asks. Mrs. Barker does not reprimand him in any way, but matter-of-factly replies, "Yes. Basket, please," and gestures to the waste basket before resuming her discussion.

At such moments during Group Time early in the year, Yakov came across as an actor blissfully unaware of making his entrance during the wrong scene. He seemed oblivious to norms for classroom behavior that other children took for granted, and showed no signs of focusing his attention on the group activity the teacher was conducting. If one were looking to derive a picture of Yakov's distinctive inquiry self from his behavior at Group Time, one might conclude that his preferred language-and-action ways struck a discordant note with the teacher's agenda, and did not usually serve as positive personal resources for language learning and making sense of curriculum. Whereas Inga and Pierre had distinctive and persistent ways of turning toward the teacher's topics, Yakov often did not turn toward them at all.

Yakov seemed to begin school at a different starting point than the other case study children. He displayed less receptive and expressive skill in English than the others, except Robert. This may have accounted for some of his lack of engagement with Group Time activities beyond the most scripted and predictable, such as fingerplays and circle games. But he also came into school without showing any awareness of having to live up to anyone else's expectations, of having to "fit in."

SEEKING INTERACTION WITH
THE TEACHER

For Yakov, a prime expectation in coming to school seemed to be that he would share *his* thoughts, *his* experiences, *his* enjoyment of his possessions, and *his* preferences and intentions with a receptive adult. The way he started the morning on Day 6 was typical of this. His blue eyes were bright and his face open and confident as he started to talk to me earnestly, all the while gesturing to his shirt, pants, and shoes. Moving on to share the same message about his clothes with Mrs. Barker, he left in his wake the clear impression that he loved to talk and was comfortable accessing adults in school. All of this he did in Russian, which was the language he used to address everyone in school for the first several weeks. Until his painful misunderstanding on Day 7 about taking toys home, he seemed quite confident that the school world would accommodate *his* modes of expression.

Mrs. Barker did not appear ruffled when Yakov remained detached from many Group Time activities. She did not label him "uncooperative," nor did she respond to him deliberately in ways which marginalized him or embarrassed him in the eyes of his peers. If he was restlessly prowling around on the outskirts of the group, she would give him a choice: "Yakov, sit in your chair or on the floor." She would often address him by name to refocus his attention, and waited a whole month before becoming more insistent about his sitting with the class during Group Time.

Mrs. Barker gave Yakov time to approach making sense of kindergarten in his own way and exhibited patience with the uncertain timetable of his getting into English and into her curriculum. As already described in Chapter 3, Yakov chose to begin establishing intersubjectivity using English in the one arena with which he seemed most comfortable, one-to-one interactions with adults. Mrs. Barker tried to meet him on his own terms for those many brief encounters, allowing him to take the lead in structuring the content. Her responsiveness enabled Yakov to use his ease with adults as a valuable resource for getting into English.

This chapter describes how Yakov's preferred language-and-action way of frequently checking in with the teacher involved two tendencies: a gradual expansion of task-related talk and an increasing ability to express his preferences and intentions clearly in English. I discuss particular points of contact between these tendencies and the teacher's curriculum that coincided with the teacher's agenda for his learning.

EXPANDING THE FOCUS OF INTERACTIONS

Yakov's seeking out one-to-one interaction with the teacher persisted throughout the year, and the purposes for which he used English in those encounters became more varied. By Day 29, Yakov had begun to expand the focus of his English interactions with the teacher from concrete objects to classroom routines. By that time, the range and sequence of kindergarten activities had become more predictable to Yakov. When the class would line up on the way from or to the classroom, he would methodically try to confirm his prediction of what was coming next by addressing Mrs. Barker with a one-word question: "Lunch?" or "Gym?" or "Eat? Snack?" The reader may also recall from Chapter 5 his confirmation checks about getting dressed to go home.

Yakov soon expanded the purposes for which he used English with the teacher to include clarifying his understanding of the directions for a task. He first did this with the support of his color vocabulary. For instance, when the children were doing art work with crayons and collage materials in blue, black, or brown only, Yakov approached the teacher with a yellow crayon and asked, "Yellow?" The teacher intuitively knew that this was not just a labeling question and replied, "No, blue, brown, and black." Next, Yakov fished out a blue crayon and held it up to her, and Mrs. Barker responded, "Yes, blue. Good boy."

Yakov's task-related talk then extended to math activities, which fit well with his enjoyment of sorting materials, ranging from the little manipulatives in a count-and-sort game to toys, stray pencils, and crayons at cleanup time. He even lined up potato sticks in his lunch box into neat rows. By Day 55, Yakov was asking for step-by-step confirmation that he was doing the math exercises correctly. He devised an economical script for discussing which math sets to circle and which to cross out by using a combination of gesture, the referential pronoun *dis* [this], and the terms *circle* and *X*.

YAKOV: Mrs. Barker. Mrs. Barker. (points to one example) Circle.
(points to another) Circle. (points to a third) Circle.
T: Yes.
. . .
YAKOV: Mrs. Barker, X?
T: Yes.
YAKOV: Dis X.
T: Yes.

Later in the year, on Day 90 and Day 108, Yakov incorporated relational and conceptual language into his vocabulary very clearly to get at the essence of specific math exercises, once he understood them. For example, on Day 90 he showed me a follow-the-dots ditto and traced one of the lines backward with his finger from a higher number to a lower number. After I told him, "Start with 1. Go to 2," he began checking in, waiting for a confirming nod each time he connected another dot:

> YAKOV: After 3, 4. (looks at me, connects two dots) After 4, 5.
> (looks at me, draws a line to the next dot) After 5 comes 6.
> (looks at me, continues the line) After 7, 8.

Similarly, on Day 108, pointing at two trees the same height in his workbook, he told me, "Same. Same. Trees same. Hey, same."

A PATH TO CURRICULUM PAVED WITH *HIS* INTENTIONS

On Day 55, which marked the initiation of Yakov's "math talk" discussed above, he also became particularly persistent about expressing his own intentions and preferences to the teacher. At times, he seemed to be making a confirmation check that what he wanted to do was okay to do. At other times, he seemed bent on making it very clear to the teacher that he had specific preferences.

First, Yakov started describing what he was going to do. Following through on the teacher's instructions that those finished with their snack might take a book, Yakov informed her, "Mrs. Barker, go /gyet/ books." When he came back from the bookshelf, he announced, "I have two books. Two books." A little later, he noticed the cash register in the house corner, and checked in once with me and once with Mrs. Barker about using it.

> YAKOV: (to Res) (pointing to open cash register) Open dis. Close
> me? (closes it)
> . . .
> YAKOV: (to T) Mrs. Barker, I close dis. Mrs. Barker, I open dis?

Yakov also started to make use of the expression "I want" in making known his preferences. While working on an art project on Day 81, he stated, "No. I won't color with that color. I want yellow. I find yellow." He also was very firm about stating his preference to follow his own interests, when the teacher encouraged children to try out a retractable tape measure that she had introduced in relation to the book *Short Train, Long Train* (Asch, 1992).

DANIEL: (to T) I wanna play dis [tape measure]. I wann play dis.
YAKOV: (to T, loudly and emphatically) I wanna play *my* toy.
T: (to Yakev) Okay. That's fine too. . . .

Expressing Intentions and Voting

In interactions such as these, what might stand out is that his intentions were often related to his own agenda, not to fulfilling the teacher's expectations. And yet, being so clear about his own intentions had its positive side. For instance, Yakov's taking his own intentions very seriously was very compatible with the teacher's agenda when it came to voting in class. Mrs. Barker used the book *Short Train, Long Train* (Asch, 1992) as the basis for providing the children with the experience of voting. She first introduced the opposites *long* and *short* with the book, in which pages of short trains, dogs, noses, and walks, among other things, folded out to become long trains, dogs, noses, and walks. She gave children turns to transform something short into something long by unfolding the page, and Yakov had the turn to make the short walk into a long walk. Then she asked the children to vote on which object from the book they wanted to select for a class drawing of a long and short version on mural paper:

T: . . . Short and long. Now tell me. Which one did you like the best? Did you like the train, or the nose, or the walk, or the tail? . . . OK, if you like the nose, stand up.

Mrs. Barker made it clear that you could vote only once. A number of children did not get that concept, but Yakov was one of the children who did. He was loyal to the long walk, for which he had had a turn. Many children chose to stand up for the picture that seemed popular, jumping on the bandwagon, so to speak, but he stuck to his original choice, even though only three children chose it.

Expressing Intentions and Social Control

Yakov's evolving tendency to make his intentions public also sometimes matched the teacher's agenda in terms of regulating his social behavior. In an episode on Day 108, Yakov expressed clearly in English to both peers and adults his intention to take something that didn't belong to him. His repeated announcements of his intentions provided an opportunity for peers and adults to influence his behavior. During a math workbook activity, Janine discovered glue leaking in her school bag and retreated to the sink to wash it out. Meanwhile, Yakov noticed Janine's little plastic pouch lying on the table, and was moved to take it to avenge past wrongs.

> YAKOV: I take Janine's. I take da Janine. (grabs hold of the pouch)
> YAKOV: (a minute later) I take Janine. I Janine's take. Because she take my/
> FRANCIA: (to Yakov) It's Janine's. It's Janine's.
> YAKOV: (to Francia) No, she take my sticker.
> RES: (to Yakov) Mrs. Barker will be very angry if you take Janine's things. Even if she took your stickers.
> YAKOV: (to Res) She take my sticker.
> RES: (to Yakov) But you shouldn't/ if it's not nice to take your stickers, it's not nice to take her things either.
> T: (to Res) Is that Janine's thing he has there?
> RES: (to T) Yes.
> T: (to Yakov) Oh::: Yakov, it's Janine's.

Yakov goes to the sink and gives the pouch to Janine.

> JANINE: (to Yakov) Mine!
> PENNY: (to Yakov) It belongs to Janine.

Yakov's clear expression of his intentions in this episode generated feedback from both adults and peers that reinforced classroom norms and kept him out of trouble.

MILESTONES IN LANGUAGE AND PARTICIPATION

One crucial element in Yakov's making sense of kindergarten and accommodating to its norms was time. His timetable for getting into English and the curriculum seemed to be characterized by sudden "growth spurts" that signaled milestones in his developing receptive and expressive skills in English.

Tuning into Group Time Discussions

The first milestone, around Day 55, was marked by Yakov's focused responses to Group Time discussions—responses reflecting his understanding of the content. On that day, although he addressed his comments to me, they were relevant to the topic the teacher had introduced.

> In anticipation of Hanukkah, Mrs. Barker was talking about the menorah (candelabra) that Jewish families would light each

evening. When she cautioned, "You may not touch matches," Yakov turned to me and said, "My father touch a matches. My mother touch a matches."

This milestone in understanding was confirmed when Yakov contributed more directly to a group discussion later in December, on Day 63. Mrs. Barker was talking about families in preparation for making holiday cards. First she read the big book *I Love My Family* (Beal, 1991), and then started to talk about family members and "people we love."

T: (to class) Put up my [your] hand if you have a mother. I have
    one mother. (She raises her hand.)
CHILD: I have one mother.
YAKOV: I have one mother.
. . .
T: (to class) I have/ D'you have an uncle? Ah, I have one uncle.
DANIEL: I have two uncles.
OGUSAN: I have one uncle.
INGA: And I have one uncle.
YAKOV: No uncles.

There is quite a din, as children call out in an overlapping manner:

CHILD 1: I love my uncle.⎤
CHILD 2: I like uncle.   ⎥
SEVERAL CHILDREN: / (in Chinese) /⎥
YAKOV: I love my mother.   ⎦

Adopting the Demeanor of Model Student

The second milestone was marked by a change in demeanor, reflecting his greater awareness of the teacher's expectations for model student behavior at Group Time. Right after winter break, on Day 67, his whole demeanor was different. When the teacher said, "Come sit on the floor, children," he sat down in the meeting area, leaning forward expectantly. He seemed to have an air about him of "I know I am a student in this class and here is what we do." Instead of getting restless during a period when children were volunteering short narratives about gifts they had received over the holiday, he raised his hand for a turn to talk. His story was about a gift from Ogusan, a classmate whom he greatly admired.

T: Yes, Yakov.
YAKOV: Ogusan gives /sneekers/

T: (looks at me for a possible explanation)
RES: Stickers. Ogusan gives stickers.
T: (to Yakov) Did you say thank-you?
YAKOV: (enunciating carefully to Ogusan) Thank-you.

Participating: Imitation and Beyond

When Yakov tuned into some of the academic activities in class, he participated often by imitating what others had said. On Day 91, Yakov repeated both correct and incorrect suggestions offered by other children for the Letter of the Week Alphabet Chart, so it was not clear whether he understood the phonics principle. This type of participation was not treated in any derogatory way by the teacher as being a "copycat," but rather as a sign that he was beginning to want to participate actively, and that he was able to figure out enough of the English speech of those around him to be able to use it himself.

On Day 91, when the teacher read and discussed *Little Red Riding Hood* (Lippert, 1988), not all of Yakov's responses were merely imitative. At the end of the story, he imitated Ivan's response, and contributed an original one:

T: ". . . I will never again wander off the path to the forest. From
        now on I will listen to my mother. The End."
IVAN: Nice story.
T: Thank you. That's the story] of little Red Riding Hood.
YAKOV: Nice story.]
T: Now tell me, was she a good girl?
CHILD: Yes]
SEVERAL CHILDREN :   No]
T: .   Yeh, she was a good girl. But what did she/
YAKOV: The *wolf* was the bad.
T: Yes. He was bad. But what did little Red Riding Hood do wrong?

Yakov's responses reflected not only that he was tuned into what others around him were saying, but that he was actively engaged with the topic under discussion and had an opinion to contribute.

YAKOV'S RESOURCES FIND A SUPPORTIVE CONTEXT

Looking at Yakov's distinctive language-and-action ways highlights how important it was for Mrs. Barker to be sensitive to the different communicative contexts in which a child uses language in the classroom. If one were only to focus on his behavior at Group Time early in the year, one might be in danger of labeling him as uncooperative, immature, not able to focus, and too self-involved. However, if one takes into account his strategies in one-to-one interactions with adults, one gets a very different picture—a picture of a child making serious efforts to negotiate shared meanings in a new language, to come to terms with new norms, and to figure out how his intentions and preferences fit in with the teacher's agenda for schooling.

Two of Yakov's language-and-action ways that evolved into valuable personal resources for getting into English were his enjoyment of interacting with adults and his love of order. It was crucial for Yakov to be able to approach school through the channel of ready access to adults on a one-to-one basis, with the opportunity to play a major role in structuring the content of those encounters. Methodically checking in with adults was his way of developing strategies for negotiating shared meaning in English and for gaining familiarity with norms and routines. The majority of traditional ESL teaching strategies focus on helping children tune into the teacher's agenda for procedures and curriculum by making that agenda understandable. These strategies were important for Yakov, as they were for his classmates. For Yakov, however, it was equally important to learn how to articulate his *own* intentions clearly, and his efforts to do so eventually supported his increased use of English, his engagement with curriculum, and his socialization.

8

Conclusions and Implications

On Day 118, Tracy talks to me as she draws an umbrella on her spring basket.

TRACY: And I can draw a umbrella . . . I draw all by myself. My mommy help me do. . . . Cause I'm a little baby then // and my father and I can draw anything I like, so my father holded my hand I can write a umbrella!

Tracy described the guiding hand of her parents at home as a resource to help her do what she at first could not do on her own. In the ESL kindergarten, Mrs. Barker's guiding hand was present in many guises, as she supported children's efforts to do with language and curriculum what they could not originally do on their own. Theirs was a "room full of talk," a room filled with the voices of particular players in a particular classroom landscape, trying to make sense in their ESL kindergarten. A close examination of this room full of talk revealed many positive resources that teacher and children brought to and developed in their classroom.

DOCUMENTATION OF EFFORTS TO MEET CHALLENGES

Mrs. Barker and the children addressed three challenges that concern monolingual teachers in multilingual classrooms: first, establishing intersubjectivity; second, making sure that the teacher's language was accessible to the children; and third, finding a balance between teacher-fronted and peer-mediated contexts for talk that would best capitalize on teacher talk and yet make room for possible peer support for L2 learning. In both teacher-fronted and peer-mediated contexts for talk, the children and Mrs. Barker revealed a broad range of strategies for establishing intersubjectivity in terms of understanding each other's literal meanings, figuring out procedures for tasks and participation, and negotiating the relevance of children's individual approaches to the teacher's curriculum.

I have documented the many strategies that the teacher enacted to make her language accessible to the children not only in terms of their receptive skills, but in terms of their expressive skills as well. In terms of receptive skills, the children relied on the teacher's patterned language, clear lesson formats, and predictable participation structures to figure out what was going on and how to participate. In terms of expressive skills, children established links between teacher-fronted and peer-mediated activities as they appropriated the teacher's language and transformed it to fulfill a combination of academic and social purposes.

Extensive observation of children's talk in contexts where they could shape their own interaction yielded many examples of children providing each other with peer support for getting into English, speaking it more, and speaking with increasing precision. Peer support strategies are summarized in Figure 8.1. The children, using strategies associated both with good language learners and with good language facilitators, were on the giving and receiving end of peer support. By the end of the study period, all of the case study children were using increasingly complex, elaborated sentences to sustain interaction with peers and/or the teacher. Peer-mediated contexts for talk could definitely not be dismissed as downtime for L2 learning in Mrs. Barker's classroom.

MRS. BARKER'S EXPECTATIONS, BELIEFS, AND PRACTICES

Lindfors (1999) makes the point that how we characterize the children's voices that we hear depends on the background of our expectation of how they should sound in that particular situation. Monolingual teachers, so used to verbal feedback from English-speaking children, when first confronting multilingual classrooms sometimes have a difficult time visualizing the positive resources these young children bring to the table. Low expectations can affect the degree and quality of investment they make in teaching L2 learners. Before I met Mrs. Barker, I supervised two student teachers who told me that the teachers in their prekindergarten field placement "didn't like their afternoon class." When I asked why, they said "because the children don't speak English and so they don't give the teachers any feedback. It's no fun to teach them." It has since struck me that for those teachers, the non-English-speaking children were always slightly "out of focus" and not "real." Because the children did not provide verbal

STRATEGIES THAT FOSTERED PEER COMMUNICATION ACROSS LANGUAGE BACKGROUNDS

1 Using pantomime and gesturing to concrete objects to substitute for language

2 Trading onomatopoeic traffic and animal sounds in lieu of words

3 Monitoring communication in a different home language and taking a best guess to make one's own English comments contingent

4 Persistently engaging peers in conversation during a variety of activities, about a variety of things, using a variety of structures

5 Choosing familiar media characters and plots and familiar phrases from media scripts to sustain interaction

6 Appropriating teacher talk and Group Time participation structures to sustain interaction focused on shared perceptions of school routines

7 Codeswitching back and forth between English and home language to keep others in the same conversational loop

STRATEGIES TO INDUCT OTHERS INTO PLAY USING ENGLISH AS THE LINGUA FRANCA

1 Taking on authoritative roles such as teacher or doctor in dramatic play to establish English as lingua franca

2 Drawing a peer into play in English by providing a "language bath," persistently treating the play as an interactive game, describing one's own actions, bidding for attention, asking direct questions

3 Switching momentarily to home language to make sure that cospeakers understood the play taking place in English

OTHER STRATEGIES PROVIDING OR DRAWING ON PEER SUPPORT

1 Imitating English speech of more fluent peer

2 Enlisting more literate peer as coreader

3 Drawing on minireservoirs of circulating vocabulary for language practice

4 Supplying corrective feedback

5 Egging on a peer to react more, thereby pushing peer to elaborate or elaborating oneself

6 Extending each other's imagery in English

Figure 8.1. Peer support strategies for fostering communication across language backgrounds and for getting into speaking English.

feedback, they were not clearly visible to the teachers as effective communicators and significant actors on the classroom stage.

Mrs. Barker had a very different set of expectations, and the strategies she enacted in establishing intersubjectivity, providing access to her language, and making room for peer support were compatible with these expectations. First, before the children could give her verbal feedback in English, she did not regard the children primarily as "limited English proficient." Rather, she treated them as whole personalities, with intentions, preferences, interests, feelings, and unique language-and-action ways. In the very first ball games early in the year, she was able to give them the message that she knew they had opinions, even though the opinions were expressed nonverbally as variations in the ball game. She viewed them as experienced communicators who were making efforts to expand their repertoire of communicative competence to include English.

Second, she held to the expectation, consonant with an interactionist framework for L2 acquisition, that the children had a desire to communicate and would benefit from a social environment where opportunities to do so would abound. Mrs. Barker built in opportunities for children to talk to each other from the very beginning, using whatever means they were most comfortable with, including use of their home languages. She assumed that the children already knew how to make meaning in one language, and saw no good reason why they should have to put meaning making on hold while learning a new language. This accounted for her allowing a wide latitude for the types of strategies children used to establish intersubjectivity. In Mrs. Barker's classroom, the emphasis was on negotiation of shared meaning rather than strictly on the forms of language. There were no silent children in Mrs. Barker's classroom. The broad range of contexts for talk accommodated a variety of receptive and expressive skill levels in L2, and to a large extent allowed for children's individual preferences as to when, why, and with whom they would talk, using English or their home language. Over time, the children found many ways to negotiate shared meaning that involved putting English to a variety of uses.

One of the contexts for talk that Mrs. Barker tried to structure into each day was some time when she would be available for one-to-one interactions with children. She was always making the rounds when children were working at their tables on tasks, whether these were art activities or more academic math or literacy activities. Thus these were often the times that Tracy and others would ask her questions or request more materials, check in for approval, or just volunteer a narrative. These times proved particularly important to Yakov.

Third, Mrs. Barker recognized that, although all the children were L2 learners, they came into her class with varying receptive and expressive skill levels in English that would be manifested in different timetables for tuning into particular activities. Since Group Time provided maximum exposure to the teacher's English, Mrs. Barker tried to ensure that every child—no matter how shy, how unaccustomed to functioning as part of a large group, or how unfamiliar with English—would be able to understand and respond to some aspect of Group Time activities from early in the year. To this end, she provided a range of activities from very predictable scripted games to open-ended discussions. Topical themes, such as family, animals, body parts, and colors, were periodically recycled along with core vocabulary, so that "late bloomers" didn't miss out.

Fourth, Mrs. Barker expected that she would continually have to integrate the teaching of language and content. In my introductory chapter, in discussing challenges facing monolingual teachers confronted with multilingual classrooms, I alluded to the fact that the teachers can no longer take for granted teaching content *through* language. Mrs. Barker always kept in mind that teaching language and *through* language went hand in hand. Her accommodation of Inga's persistent questioning about the whys and wherefores of tasks during task demonstrations led to a highlighting for peers of key vocabulary, especially as Inga incorporated more specific descriptive vocabulary into her questions. Those questions were so welcome because Mrs. Barker never forgot that the point of the demonstrations was not just showing children how to do tasks, but getting them to understand and use task-related language.

Fifth, Mrs. Barker recognized that establishing intersubjectivity didn't just have a cognitive dimension, but also an emotional one. It can be very tiring for new speakers of a language to conduct themselves in that language for sustained periods. In Mrs. Barker's classroom, where everyone had to make so much effort to understand and be understood, moments when it didn't feel hard to understand each other felt very good. Thus, for example, the daily ritual of an exaggerated "waking and stretching" at the end of Rest Time (as described in Chapter 3), united the whole class in precious moments of shared understanding of an insider joke. Using L2 also involves taking the risk of making mistakes in public. Opportunities for responding in unison during scripted games and for calling out answers reduced the risk of exposure for imperfect English and gave plenty of opportunity for children to begin to savor the sounds and feel of English in their mouths with anonymity. Mrs. Barker also expected children to imitate each other's English responses. She took it as a positive sign that they were tuning into the language around them. Sometimes chiming in with the same response as one's peers was a way of saying "this discussion is relevant to my experience too," as when Yakov chimed in with "I have one mother."

Sixth, Mrs. Barker did not expect all children to react in some one ideal way to her curriculum activities. She regarded it as an ordinary, everyday occurrence that individual children would display unique ways of approaching her curriculum, including L2 learning. She seemed to assume also what Donato (2000) deemed a central concern in sociocultural theory regarding L2 learners: "that learners actively transform their world and do not merely conform to it" (p. 46). Mrs. Barker expected that as children engaged with curriculum activities, they would to some extent transform what took place, and she was comfortable with responding by improvising on her lesson scripts. She seemed to acknowledge intuitively what Dyson (1999) urges teachers not to dismiss, namely, resources that children themselves deem relevant to school tasks. Mrs. Barker was thus able to view Pierre's sound effects, Inga's wisecracks and persistent questions, and Yakov's methodical checking in about crayon colors as relevant language-and-action ways of making sense of the curriculum. Her legitimizing of their language-and-action ways benefited them individually, as it led them to increased precision of expression or a sharper academic focus; and in the case of Inga and Pierre, it also showcased the teacher's meanings for the benefit of their peers. Mrs. Barker also was not stymied or put off by Yakov's initial lack of engagement with much of her curriculum, and made room in her interactive space for *his* preferences for one-to-one contact with adults and for *his* intentions to be heard.

Seventh, Mrs. Barker did not define the children only in terms of how they related to *her* concerns. She did not view them only as revolving in orbit around her. She was able to picture them as being at the center of their own universe. For instance, when Robert would pick and choose whether to engage in particular activities or tasks, she described him as "fiercely independent," rather than "uncooperative" or "unmotivated." Based on this orientation toward the children, Mrs. Barker balanced Group Time with many other more informal contexts for talk that were not teacher-directed in the way that Group Time was. It was in those peer-mediated contexts that she allowed children to appropriate her language, her procedural talk, her read-alouds, her lesson formats, and her scripts for routines, and to recontextualize them for their own social and academic purposes. Some of the children's appropriation of the teacher's language was anticipated and fostered by Mrs. Barker, as she deliberately enacted strategies to encourage children to use task-related language at their tables during writing, math, and art activities. But often, in unanticipated ways, the children adapted her teacher talk and participation structures as interim scripts to sustain their play in English or as authoritative texts to support their efforts to master academic activities that Mrs. Barker had modeled, such as read-alouds and math problems.

   The expanded definition of establishing intersubjectivity that emerged
in this study made room for recognition of children's and teacher's resources that might otherwise go unnoticed. That expanded definition included children's and teacher's efforts to construct together a frame of
reference in which not only literal language meanings, but the hows and
whys of activities were negotiated, as discussed in Chapter 3. The expanded
definition also took into account children's individual language-and-
action ways of making sense of and in English, and making the teacher's
language and literacy goals for them more personally relevant, as discussed
in Chapters 4 through 7. Recognition of those resources required looking
beyond the boundaries of the particular "imaginative universe" (Dyson,
1993, 1999) defined by an interactionist framework of L2 acquisition to
include sets of collaborative relationships that are often left unrecognized
or unexplored. I looked at the details of peer interactions among ELLs in
a range of classroom contexts and identified very context-specific ways in
which children collaborated and supported each other's L2 learning. I also
documented links between children's social and academic purposes, between negotiating shared meanings in a literal sense and language-and-
action ways of turning toward a topic, and between teacher-fronted and
peer-mediated classroom contexts for communication.

SOCIAL ENERGY FUELING PEER SUPPORT

Freedom for children to shape their own interaction provided an opportunity for their social energy to fuel much of their effort to interact with peers
in English. It was in some of these informal contexts for talk, where children could pursue their own agendas, that children manifested the most
peer support for L2 learning and use. Much peer interaction in English
sprouted when children were just sitting around at their tables at Snack Time
or Rest Time, with no all-consuming teacher-imposed agenda. For Inga,
Tracy, and Jerry, minding each other's business and a shared focus on snacks,
drink boxes, art materials, name labels, and other concrete referents at their
table led to interesting and increasingly complex language collaborations.
In egging each other on, they pushed each other to elaborate and clarify
their English. It was frequently during Play Time, when children had the
most choice of interactive partners, that efforts were made to draw more
children into English-speaking play. This was certainly true of the efforts
made by Inga and Tracy, and was also true for the efforts made by Daniel to
draw Robert into play in English toward the end of the study.
   Anyone could own the words in Mrs. Barker's classroom, and Mrs.
Barker gave the children space to transform them in ways that often re-

sulted in parodies of her teaching, sometimes with a note of irreverence toward authority. Mrs. Barker did not squelch these play scenarios, and through them children had opportunities to expand their linguistic capital. The wide range of contexts for talk and the wide latitude for strategies of negotiating shared meaning seemed to give children room for "talking to each other, playing with each other, fighting with each other, and loving each other" (Ashton-Warner, 1963, quoted in Dyson, 1993). This togetherness seemed to generate a degree of peer support for each other's L2 learning which I have not seen reported elsewhere in the ESL literature.

IMPLICATIONS OF PEER COLLABORATION

Children collaborated with peers of both like and different backgrounds to help each other do many things with English they could not originally do on their own, bearing out the notion of scaffolding by a more capable peer. A combination of children's individual resources and the particulars of the specific learning situation played a large role in who was giver and who was receiver of support in any given context. That fact suggests that what particular children have to offer each other in support of L2 learning cannot be boiled down to labels such as *native speaker* and *English language learner*. The example of Penny's support for Inga in the *Brown Bear, Brown Bear* reading episode is a case in point. Penny derived support from familiarity with the authoritative text of Mrs. Barker's read-aloud, and in turn was able to use this to model appropriate textual language for Inga, whose literacy knowledge was less sophisticated.

Peer support manifested in Inga's interactions with Jerry and Tracy also involved a combination of individual resources and particulars of the situations. Jerry and Tracy benefited from Inga's superior English fluency, and her flair for pantomime supported sustained interaction with them as they explored the pleasures of sharing their common perceptions of school routines. All three of them drew support for this sharing from what Johnson (1994) terms the *contextual* sphere, in this instance their common social experiences of classroom routines and of family relationships.

A set of strategies that highlighted a resource used by the children, but unavailable to the teacher, was codeswitching between English and their respective home languages. Children used codeswitching for many different purposes. Tracy sometimes would translate key English phrases to her Chinese-speaking playmates in the house corner, to clue them in to her predominantly English role-plays. Jerry or Inga would occasionally translate a peer's home language statement into English to keep other peers in the conversational loop. Jerry switched to Chinese with Tracy, who preferred English, when he wanted to tell her an insider joke about Chinese New Year.

Implications for Cooperative Learning

There were many instances in children's appropriation of the teacher's language where their activity and interaction served a combination of social and academic purposes. This would suggest to me that perhaps, at least at the kindergarten level, there could be considerable overlap between cognitive-academic language proficiency and basic interpersonal communication skills, often referred to as CALP and BICS (Cummins, 1979). For example, the scenario of the drink box family improvised by Jerry, Inga, and Tracy was a pleasurable social interaction with a number of academic elements. It had many ingredients of a build-a-story activity that teachers sometimes undertake with a wordless picture book. In a build-a-story activity, each child gets to add to the story by adding verbal text to the next illustration in the picture book. To do this successfully, children have to have a sense of sequence of events, and of qualities of characters. They also need to be listening very carefully to each other in order to contribute the next step to building a coherent story. All these elements were present in the drink box scenario, where children were learning to participate in English in a contingent conversation.

In higher school grades, cooperative learning is a type of context that requires both BICS and CALP. In Mrs. Barker's kindergarten, the children's informal collaborations during Table Activities did not take place in a framework of cooperative learning; rather they occurred in a framework more similar to the enhanced individual work described by Johnson (1994), in which children worked on individual tasks, but were free to draw informally on their peers as resources. However, the children did display some of the skills essential for cooperative learning, such as sustaining a shared focus and listening actively to each other. They also exhibited behaviors and skills that would be needed in order to maximize the language-learning benefits of cooperative learning activities: behaviors such as pushing each other to clarify and elaborate, and skills such as providing corrective feedback. Since the children's spontaneous collaborations involved many of the skills that are necessary for engaging in cooperative learning activities, it would be worthwhile to investigate the potential of cooperative learning activities as a catalyst for L2 learning in this type of ESL setting, where L2 learners are dependent on each other for interaction. In such endeavors, children could draw on two kinds of support to link cooperative learning activities to more teacher-directed contexts. First, children could draw support from textual spheres, such as teacher read-alouds and lesson scripts. Second, children could draw support from contextual spheres, with more emphasis on their shared social understandings of routines and participation structures.

Implications of Constraints on Peer Support

In Mrs. Barker's classroom, it seemed important for children not to be isolated for long periods with peers only of their own language background. Certainly, Robert, surrounded by fellow Cantonese tablemates, took a long time to explore ways of negotiating shared meaning in English. In many schools, administrators lump together all speakers of one language background in one class for an ESL rather than a bilingual program. If a true bilingual program is not an option, it would seem to me counterproductive to isolate all children of one language background together in a single classroom. The population of the class should be more diverse, so as to make it more likely that children will try to use English as a lingua franca to converse.

THE IMPORTANCE OF A BROAD RANGE OF CONTEXTS FOR TALK

In order to capitalize on children's capacity for peer support, providing a broad range of contexts for communication seemed essential in Mrs. Barker's classroom. The kind of curriculum that Mrs. Barker presented in her kindergarten included a set of activities that many teachers will instantly recognize—activities such as the calendar and Letter of the Week. In some early childhood classrooms with such a traditional program, instructional contexts are limited only to alternating cycles of teacher-directed Group Time and the isolating quiet of independent seatwork. Such classrooms do not accommodate the children's collaborative strategies for getting into English reported here. If teachers and students are to work together to create equal access to a learning community in which English is spoken, room for talk in that shared language over a wide range of communicative contexts will be an essential classroom component.

The children in this case study all began to access an expanding pool of English and a network of English users in Mrs. Barker's classroom. However, L2 acquisition research tells us that it may take at least 5 years for the children from this ESL kindergarten to gain full academic proficiency in English (Collier, 1987). For the bulk of that time, most will be in mainstream classrooms. Administrators need to set the tone in their schools for classrooms that offer L2 learners a wide range of choices for participating, negotiating shared meanings, and displaying their growing communicative competence in English.

CONSISTENCY, DIVERSITY, AND THE ART OF TEACHING

To accommodate the different children in her classroom, Mrs. Barker created consistency, yet planned for diversity at the same time; she established regularities, yet made room for spontaneity. Children could rely on the consistency of lesson formats, clearly established participation structures for particular activities, and scripts associated with certain routines. And they could also find some aspect of curriculum with which to connect on a continuum from highly scripted to very open-ended verbal interactions. Teacher talk and its regularities had an impact far beyond its original contexts because children had the freedom to export it from its original contexts and transform it.

Establishing consistency and planning for diversity are broad teaching strategies that apply far beyond this particular classroom and have implications for preparing teachers to work in multilingual classrooms. Some of the strategies that Mrs. Barker enacted, such as rephrasing children's responses and including scripted games in her curriculum, could be considered part of the science of teaching. They involve learning and understanding certain skills, and applying them under fairly predictable circumstances. However, sensitively responding to the ways that children turn toward curriculum requires going beyond any particular blueprint for teaching. It requires teacher improvisation, part of the art of teaching. The source of such improvisation is not mastery of a particular skill, but a vision of children that allows for diversity, spontaneity, and recognition of the positive potential in what L2 learners bring into the classroom. This potential includes, among other elements, their history as effective communicators in a first language, and their social energy.

One might ask, "How do you derive a lesson from another teacher's improvisations? After all, the spontaneous emergence of an insider joke about Rest Time is rooted in the events of one particular classroom." I would answer that what one takes away from that improvisation is the idea of institutionalizing the savoring of the moment in that ritual "wake and stretch," so that children can experience again and again a sense of shared understanding.

A portrait of Mrs. Barker—her expectations, beliefs, and strategies—does not stand for every monolingual teacher in a multilingual classroom, just as portraits of Inga, Pierre, or other case study children—their individual language-and-action ways, their preferences, and their personal resources—are not representative of all ELLs in multilingual classrooms. But these very particular examples from a very specific site have implications for early childhood teachers who wish to structure their learning environments so that everyone can own the words.

One of Inga's questions about the basket-making activity, and indeed about most activities, was "Wha' we gonna do /wid/ it?" I think that is an important question to ask about English in an ESL kindergarten. What are children going to do with English? How do they figure it out? What structures in the daily program support its uses? And what makes it seem relevant to the children? In Mrs. Barker's kindergarten, we have seen one set of possibilities for a communication-rich environment for getting into English and speaking it better, with the teacher's strategies, children's resources, and children's social life providing a supportive context.

Transcription Conventions

T	Teacher (Mrs. Barker).
Res	Researcher.
( )	Description of the context of an utterance, such as accompanying physical gesture of speaker.
[ ]	Implied information supplied by transcriber—information that would be needed to make sense of the utterance.
– – –	A pause by the speaker. The more dashes, the longer the pause.
. . .	Speech that was transcribed, but not included in the example.
/	Self-corrections.
/ /	Inaudible part of an utterance.
/brager/	Researcher's interpretation of a mispronounced attempt at an English word: e.g., /brager/ for "bigger."
:	A colon indicates the preceding sound has been lengthened. The more colons, the more prolonged the elongation.
YES	Words in SMALL CAPITALS indicate original utterance in the child's home language has been translated for the transcription.
? !	Question marks and exclamation points were used when they helped convey the prosodic quality of an utterance.
very	Words receiving particular stress were italicized.
mel-ting	Hyphen between syllables indicates each syllable was pronounced very distinctly and deliberately.

]   Overlapping speech.

"text"   Utterance in quotation marks is part of a text (as from a story-
                     book) being read by the teacher.

'moi'   Home language words enclosed in single quotation marks.

References

Bakhtin, M. (1986). *Speech genres and other late essays*. Austin: University of Texas Press.

Ballenger, C. (1999). *Teaching other people's children: Literacy and learning in a bilingual classroom*. New York: Teachers College Press.

Cazden, C. B. (1988). *Classroom discourse: The language of teaching and learning*. Portsmouth, NH: Heinemann.

Chesterfield, R., Chesterfield, K. B., Hayes-Latimer, K., & Chavez, R. (1983). The influence of teachers and peers on second language acquisition in bilingual preschool programs. *TESOL Quarterly, 17*(3), 401–419.

Collier, V. P. (1987). Age and rate of acquisition of second language for academic purposes. *TESOL Quarterly, 21*(4), 617–641.

Corsaro, W. A. (1981). Entering the child's world: Research strategies for field entry and data collection in a preschool setting. In J. Green & C. Wallat (Eds.), *Ethnography and language in educational settings* (pp. 117–145). Norwood, NJ: Ablex.

Cumming, A. (2000). *Second language education in schools in Canada*. Manuscript submitted to the Center for Applied Linguistics, Washington, DC. Available on-line: http://www.oise.utoronto.ca/MLC/draft.html

Cummins, J. (1979). Cognitive / academic language proficiency, linguistic interdependence, the optimal age question, and some other matters. *Working Papers on Bilingualism, 19*, 197–205.

Cummins, J. (1994). Knowledge, power, and identity in teaching ESL. In F. Genesee (Ed.), *Educating second language children: The whole child, the whole curriculum, the whole community* (pp. 33–58). New York: Cambridge University Press.

Dixon, G., & Fraser, S. (1986). Social behaviours of children in a multicultural preschool. *TESL Canada Journal, 3*(2), 33–40.

Donato, R. (2000). Sociocultural contributions to understanding the foreign and second language classroom. In J. P. Lantolf (Ed.), *Sociocultural theory and second language learning* (pp. 27–50). Oxford: Oxford University Press.

Dyson, A. H. (1987). The value of "time off task": Young children's spontaneous talk and deliberate text. *Harvard Educational Review, 57*(4), 395–420.

Dyson, A. H. (1989). *The multiple worlds of child writers: Friends learning to write.* New York: Teachers College Press.

Dyson, A. H. (1993). *Social worlds of children learning to write in an urban primary school.* New York: Teachers College Press.

Dyson, A. H. (1999). Transforming transfer: Unruly children, contrary texts, and the persistence of the pedagogical order. *Review of Research in Education, 24,* 141–171. Washington, DC: American Educational Research Association

Ellis, R. (1983). Formulaic speech in early classroom second language development. In J. Handscombe, (Ed.), *ON TESOL '83: The question of control* (pp. 53–65). Washington, DC: TESOL (Teachers of English to Speakers of Other Languages).

Enright, D. S. (1991). Tapping the peer interaction resource. In M. E. McGroarty & C. J. Faltis (Eds.), *Languages in school and society: Policy and pedagogy* (pp. 209–232). Berlin: Mouton de Gruyter.

Erickson, F., & Shultz, J. (1981). When is a context? Some issues and methods in the analysis of social competence. In J. L. Green & C. Wallat (Eds.), *Ethnography and language in educational settings* (pp. 147–160). Norwood, NJ: Ablex.

Ervin-Tripp, S. (1991). Play in language development. In B. Scales, M. Almy, A. Nicolopoulou, & S. Ervin-Tripp (Eds.), *Play and the social context of development in early care and education* (pp. 84–97). New York: Teachers College Press.

Fassler, R. (1998). "Let's do it again!": Peer collaboration in picture book reading among ESL kindergarten children. *Language Arts, 75*(3), 202–210.

Genishi, C. (1989). Observing the second language learner: An example of teachers' learning. *Language Arts, 66*(5), 509–515.

Gomez, B. (1987). "Friends gotta talk": An ethnographic study of behavioral patterns exhibited by young children in the process of acquiring English as a second language (Doctoral dissertation, Georgia State University, 1987). *Dissertation Abstracts International, 48-07,* 1651A.

Gregory, E. (1997). *One child, many worlds: Early learning in multicultural communities.* New York: Teachers College Press.

Hickman, J. (1983). Everything considered: Response to literature in an elementary school setting. *Journal of Research and Development in Education, 16*(3), 8–13.

Hirschler, J. A. (1991). Preschool children's help to second language learners (peer help, social interaction) (Doctoral dissertation, Harvard University, 1991). *Dissertation Abstracts International, 52-06,* 2051A.

Information, Reporting and Technology Services. State Education Department. (2001). *Racial/ethnic distribution of public school students and staff, 2000–2001.* Albany: State University of New York.

Johnson, D. M. (1994). Grouping strategies for second language learners. In F. Genesee (Ed.), *Educating second language children: The whole child, the whole curriculum, the whole community* (pp. 183–211). New York: Cambridge University Press.

Kagan, S. L., & Garcia, E. E. (1991). Educating culturally and linguistically diverse preschoolers: Moving the agenda. *Early Childhood Research Quarterly, 6*(3), 411–425.

Kiefer, B. Z. (1986). The child and the picture book: Creating live circuits. *Children's Literature Association Quarterly, 11*(2), 63–68.

Lindfors, J. W. (1999). *Children's inquiry: Using language to make sense of the world.* New York: Teachers College Press.

Litowitz, B. E. (1993). Deconstruction in the zone of proximal development. In E. Forman, N. Minick, & C. A. Stone (Eds.), *Contexts for learning: Sociocultural dynamics in children's development* (pp. 184–196). New York: Oxford University Press.

McGroarty, M. (1989). The benefits of cooperative learning arrangements in second language instruction. *NABE: The Journal of the National Association for Bilingual Education, 13,* 127–133.

Office of English Language Learners. (2001). *Facts and figures 2000–2001: Answers to frequently asked questions about English Language Learners (ELLs) and bilingual/ESL programs.* New York: New York City Board of Education.

Philips, S. U. (1972). Participant structures and communicative competence: Warm Springs children in community and classroom. In C. B. Cazden, V. John, & D. Hymes (Eds.), *Functions of language in the classroom* (pp. 370–394). New York: Teachers College Press.

Pica, T. (1994). Questions from the language classroom: Research perspectives. *TESOL Quarterly, 28*(1), 49–79.

Pica, T., Lincoln-Porter, F., Paninos, D., & Linnell, J. (1996). Language learners' interaction: How does it address the input, output, and feedback needs of L2 learners? *TESOL Quarterly, 30*(1), 59–84.

Saville-Troike, M. (1985). Cultural input in second language learning. In S. M. Gass & C. G. Madden (Eds.), *Input in second language acquisition* (pp. 51–58). Rowley, MA: Newbury House.

Saville-Troike, M. (1987). Dilingual discourse: The negotiation of meaning without a common code. *Linguistics, 25*(1), 81–106.

Swain, M. (1985). Communicative competence: some roles of comprehensible input and comprehensible output in its development. In S. M. Gass & C. G. Madden (Eds.), *Input in second language acquisition* (pp. 235–253). Rowley, MA: Newbury House.

Swain, M., & Lapkin, S. (1989). Canadian immersion and adult second language teaching: What's the connection? *Modern Language Journal, 73*(2), 150–159.

Tabors, P. O. (1997). *One child, two languages.* Baltimore: Paul H. Brookes.

Tan, A. (1989). *The Joy Luck Club.* New York: Putnam.

Trueba, H. T. (1981–82). The meaning and use of context in ethnographic research: Implications for validity. *NABE: The Journal of the National Association for Bilingual Education, 6*(2 & 3), 21–34.

Urzua, C. (1989). I grow for a living. In P. Rigg & V. G. Allen (Eds.), *When they don't all speak English* (pp. 15–38). Urbana, IL: National Council of Teachers of English.

Wells, C. G. (1981). *Learning through interaction: the study of language development*. New York: Cambridge University Press.

Wong Fillmore, L. (1982). Instructional language as linguistic input: Second language learning in classrooms. In L. C. Wilkinson (Ed.), *Communicating in the classroom* (pp. 283–296). New York: Academic.

Wong Fillmore, L. (1985). When does teacher talk work as input? In S. M. Gass & C. G. Madden (Eds.), *Input in second language acquisition* (pp. 17–50). Rowley, MA: Newbury House.

Bibliography of Children's Books

Aker, S. (1990). *What comes in 2's, 3's, & 4's*. New York: Simon & Schuster Books for Young Readers.

Asch, F. (1992). *Short train, long train*. New York: Scholastic.

Beal, K. (1991). *Here it's winter—A multicultural sing-along big book*. Reading, MA: Addison Wesley.

Beal, K. (1991) *I love my family. A multicultural sing-along big book*. Boston: Addison-Wesley Longman.

Carle, E. (1987). *The tiny seed*. Boston: Picture Book Studio.

Goldilocks and the three bears (Level A) (K. Schmit, Illust.). (1989). Reading, MA: Addison Wesley.

Hoban, T. (1990). *Exactly the opposite*. New York: Trib Club.

Kalan, R. (1989). *Jump, frog, jump!* New York: Morrow.

Kightley, R. (1986). *Opposites*. Boston: Little Brown.

Lippert, M. H. (1988). *Little Red Riding Hood: A German folktale*. New York: Macmillan.

Martin, B., Jr. (1983). *Brown Bear, Brown Bear, what do you see?* New York: Holt.

Mattern, J. (1992). *Young Martin Luther King, Jr.: "I have a dream."* Mahwah, NJ: Troll.

Melser, J., & Cowley, J. (1980). *Three little ducks* (D. Cowe, Illust.). New Zealand: Shortland Publications.

The farmer and the beet (Level A) (J. Wallner, Illust.). (1989). Reading, MA: Addison Wesley.

The farmer in the dell—A singing game (M. M. Rae, Illust.). (1988). Hong Kong: Scholastic.

The three little pigs (Level A). (1989). Reading, MA: Addison Wesley.

Index

About the Author

Rebekah Fassler received her M.A. in Cultural Anthropology from Columbia University and her M.S. in Education from the Bank Street College of Education. She has taught young children aged 3 through 6 in early childhood settings and in music and movement classes, and has worked as a teacher educator since 1979. She received her Ed.D. from Teachers College, Columbia University in 1995 and is currently an associate professor in the School of Education at St. John's University, where she coordinates the Early Childhood Master's Program. Dr. Fassler's research in oral communication and emergent literacy in multilingual early childhood classrooms has been published in the *Early Childhood Research Quarterly, Language Arts,* and *Childhood Education.* She has also published research about teacher education students' concepts of developmentally appropriate practice.

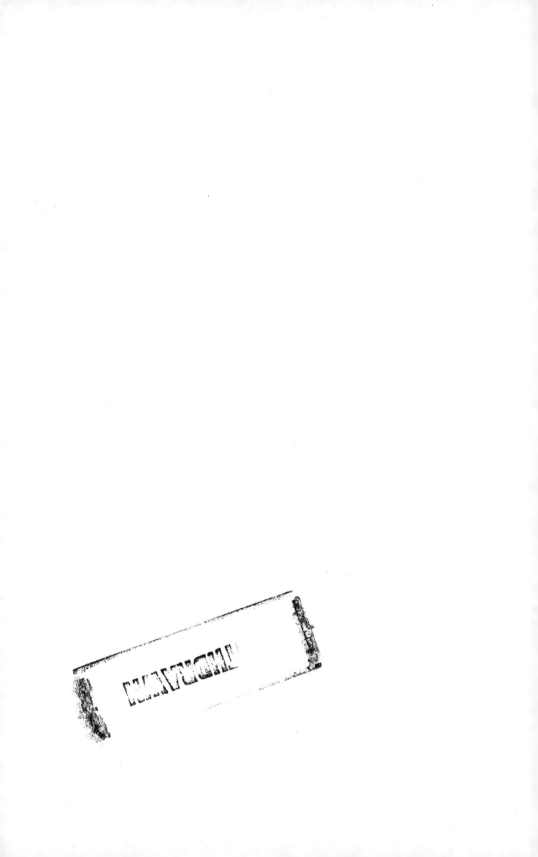